D0290343

the concept of meaninglessness

the concept of meaninglessness

Edward Erwin

THE  JOHNS HOPKINS PRESS   Baltimore and London

Copyright © 1970 by The Johns Hopkins Press
All rights reserved
Manufactured in the United States of America

The Johns Hopkins Press, Baltimore, Maryland 21218
The Johns Hopkins Press Ltd., London

Library of Congress Catalog Card Number 75–101456
International Standard Book Number 0–8018–1110–4

111.8
E73C
174468

to patricia

contents

acknowledgments

What I have learned about the topics of this book, I have learned mainly from those philosophers whose views I sometimes criticize. I hereby thank them. I have also benefited from discussions with Peter Achinstein, Sidney Gendin, Anthony Paul, Marshall Spector, and Sotirios Spiliadis.

In completing the book, I was aided by a summer fellowship from the Graduate School of the State University of New York at Stony Brook. Kenneth Arnold of The Johns Hopkins Press made many useful editorial revisions. Vere Chappell offered valuable suggestions for improving the text, and Maurice Mandelbaum has helped me in various ways. Most of all, I would like to thank Stephen F. Barker and Kingsley Price. Finally, I owe a debt of gratitude to my late father, Joseph W. Erwin.

The concept does not exist for the physicist until he has the possibility of discovering whether or not it is fulfilled in an actual case. We thus require a definition of simultaneity such that this definition supplies us with the method by means of which, in the present case, one can decide by experiment whether or not both the lightning strokes occurred simultaneously. As long as this requirement is not satisfied, I allow myself to be deceived as a physicist (and of course the same applies if I am not a physicist), when I imagine that I am able to attach a meaning to the statement of simultaneity. (I would ask the reader not to proceed until he is fully convinced on this point.)

ALBERT EINSTEIN, *Relativity: The Special and General Theory* (1916)

Now we merely have to examine any of the possible operations by which we measure time to see that all such operations are relative operations. Therefore the previous statement that absolute time does not exist is replaced by the statement that absolute time is meaningless.

P. W. BRIDGMAN, *The Logic of Modern Physics* (1927)

If I now generalize my previous statement and say, 'Stealing money is wrong,' I produce a sentence which has no factual meaning—that is, expresses no proposition which can be either true or false.

A. J. AYER, *Language, Truth and Logic* (1936)

Underlying the familiar distinction between truth and falsehood, there is a more radical distinction between significance and meaninglessness. True and false statements are both significant, but some forms of words, with the vocabulary and construction of statements, are neither true nor false, but nonsensical—and nonsensical not for reasons of wording or of grammar, but for logical reasons.

GILBERT RYLE, "Ludwig Wittgenstein" (1951)

the concept of meaninglessness

introduction

The concept of meaninglessness has played a prominent part in the development of contemporary philosophy. Indeed, questioning the meaningfulness of certain concepts, sentences, and statements became for some, until recently, the chief tactic of philosophic analysis. It is easy to see why this tactic should be considered important, for the great scandal of philosophy has always been its apparent inability to solve its problems. Some, in fact, would complain of *all* philosophy what Kant lamented of metaphysical philosophy, that "we do not find men confident of their ability to shine in other sciences venturing their reputation here, where everybody, however ignorant in other matters may deliver a final verdict, as in this domain there is as yet no standard weight and measure to distinguish sound knowledge from shallow talk."[1]

If use of the concept of meaninglessness were to fulfill its promise, then a complaint such as Kant's could now be answered, at least to some extent. By employing this concept, some philosophers thought, we could distinguish the sound knowledge from the shallow talk. The shallow talk, at least some of it, was to be eliminated, not by declaring it "false," but by ruling it "meaningless." In this way, many, although certainly not all, of the traditional disputes—about the existence of God, about Realism or Idealism, about value judgments, etc.—could be said to be settled finally and irrevocably.

---

[1] Immanuel Kant, *Prolegomena to any Future Metaphysics* (Chicago: The Open Court Publishing Company, 1909), p. 1.

But very quickly new disputes arose: disputes about what is and what is not meaningless. Resolving these new disputes, however, proved to be just as troublesome and just as embarrassing as settling the traditional disagreements. For enforcing a ruling that "X is meaningless" proved to be just as difficult as justifying such traditional assertions as "X is good" or "X is real." Until some way could be found to settle the new controversies about what is meaningless, the new solutions to the traditional problems would be of no lasting value, and the old disputes would soon begin again. The new talk of meaningless concepts and statements would have gained us nothing.

Is there a way, then, to settle disputes about what is meaningless? Or is all of this modern talk of "meaninglessness," "nonsense," "depth-absurdities," and the like just as shallow and just as vain as the metaphysical talk condemned by Kant? Many philosophers would now answer the first question negatively; many now agree that there is no way at all to justify assertions about what is meaningless. This is one form of skepticism that has arisen recently concerning the use of the concept of meaninglessness.

Such skepticism also comes in a more radical form. The more radical skeptic claims not only that the techniques of justification are all inadequate but that the very concept of meaninglessness, at least as it is employed by philosophers, is essentially defective. Philosophers have used the concept in trying to prove that certain sentences or statements could not possibly be true—something the radical skeptic argues cannot be done. Even if a sentence or statement could be shown to be meaningless, that would not demonstrate that it could not possibly be true. What is meaningless, the radical skeptic continues, is meaningless only in a given language or only at a given time; change the language or the time, and you may transform what is meaningless into what is meaningful and perhaps true.

To evaluate these two forms of skepticism, it is necessary to consider the criteria typically used by philosophers to justify their charges of "meaninglessness." There are three such criteria: the operationalist, verificationist, and type (or category) criteria. Before evaluating these criteria, however, I should make some preliminary comments about the concept I shall be discussing.

Some philosophers, but not all, sometimes use terms such as "nonsensical" or "absurd" as synonyms for "meaningless." I shall do the same. Distinctions can certainly be drawn among these three terms, and for some purposes, it is imperative that we do so. For example, in at least one very common use of the term "absurd," a very silly statement may be absurd and yet may still be meaningful. Nevertheless, for the purposes of this essay, there is no need to make the distinctions that could be made; nothing of substance will turn on my occasional use of "absurd" or "nonsensical" as substitutes for "meaningless." The reason for my allowing such substitutions is simply to make it easier to discuss the views of philosophers who prefer to use "absurd" or "nonsensical" in place of the term "meaningless."

A second point concerns the meaning, or use, of the expression "meaningless." Many contemporary philosophers have used it to mean "neither true nor false." I do think that certain difficulties arise if "meaningless" is used in exactly that way—and I shall offer in my final chapter a slightly different interpretation which escapes these difficulties—but, roughly stated, the expression as I shall be using it implies lack of truth and falsity. There are, however, other uses of the term "meaningless." It is more common in everyday speech, for example, to use "meaningless" to mean "without importance or purpose" or "without value." Thus, it is sometimes said that life is meaningless; but that is not to say that life is neither true nor false. For life, not being a linguistic item, as is a sentence or a statement, is not the kind of thing which we normally describe as either having or lacking a truth value. Moreover, when we do speak of linguistic items as being "meaningless," we do not always, or even usually, mean that they are neither true nor false. For example, the statement "The Vietnam conflict will end some day" might be described as "meaningless" on the grounds that a statement which does not say *when* the war will end is of no value. It is true, of course, that the war will end some day; but since we all know that, the statement would not be worth making in most contexts. Nevertheless, the statement is obviously true and, consequently, someone who described it as "meaningless" would probably not mean that it was "neither true nor false."

These other uses of the term "meaningless," implying lack of importance, purpose, or value, will not be discussed at all in the present essay. I do not think, however, that these other uses are illegitimate—I should make that quite clear. In a perfectly respectable use of the term "meaningless," something may be said to be meaningless without its being neither true nor false. The above statement about the war is meaningless and yet true. Although "meaningless" may be legitimately used in this way, it is not the way in which contemporary philosophers typically use it—at least not when they are attempting to solve philosophic problems. For that reason, then, and not because I question the propriety of the other, more everyday uses, I shall be discussing the concept of meaninglessness only as it is used to mean, roughly, "neither true nor false."

In discussing this concept, I hope to answer many, although not all, of the interesting questions philosophers have raised about its employment in settling philosophic disputes. For example, what does it mean to complain that a statement or sentence is meaningless? How does one justify such a complaint? Further, can sentences or statements—or neither—be said to be meaningless? Are metaphors meaningless? What is the difference between meaningless statements and contradictions? Is what is meaningless relative to a given language, to a given time—or to neither? In part, then, I hope to answer such questions and thereby to provide a somewhat general account of the philosophic use of "meaninglessness." More than that, however, I hope to show that this term, when interpreted in the manner I shall suggest, can be employed profitably by philosophers in their attempts to arbitrate philosophic disputes, despite the many recent and often trenchant criticisms of this practice.

chapter i

operationalism

The two criteria of meaninglessness most widely used in this century have been the operationalist and verificationist criteria. I shall discuss the former in this chapter and the latter in the next.

1

Operationalism (or "operationism") is a thesis most commonly associated with the Nobel Prize Laureate in physics, P. W. Bridgman. According to his original statement of the thesis, a concept is synonomous with the set of operations used in applying it in some concrete situation. Thus, Bridgman writes:

The concept of length is therefore fixed when the operations by which length is measured are fixed: that is, the concept of length involves as much as and nothing more than the set of operations by which length is determined. In general, we mean by any concept nothing more than a set of operations; *the concept is synonomous with the corresponding set of operations.*[1] (Bridgman's italics)

As formulated by Bridgman, the thesis provides a criterion for determining whether a given concept or term is meaningless; for a concept would be meaningless if it could not be defined operationally. Moreover, provision of a criterion of meaninglessness is one of the key themes of operationalism

[1] P. W. Bridgman, *The Logic of Modern Physics* (New York: The Macmillan Company, 1928), p. 5. An earlier version of operationalism can be found in the writings of Charles Sanders Peirce.

and is the theme which Bridgman himself has continued to emphasize long after rejecting or modifying other elements of his original account. Thus, in a relatively recent publication, he writes: "The fundamental idea back of an operational analysis is . . . that we do not know the meaning of a concept unless we can specify the operations which were used by us or our neighbor in applying the concept in any concrete situation."[2]

Bridgman has insisted, more than once, that he came to formulate his criterion after observing the writings and workings of his fellow physicists, particularly Albert Einstein.[3] Moreover, apart from the genesis of the original thesis, the concept of an operational definition is probably most at home in the context of experimental physics. Nevertheless, it is not in physics but in the social sciences, particularly in psychology, that the introduction of Bridgman's criterion has probably had its greatest impact. The development and growth of behaviorism, for instance, especially reflects the influence of operationalism.[4] In the other social sciences as well, Bridgman's criterion has been adopted and utilized,[5] and many social scientists, perhaps most, would probably agree that the influence of operationalism has been widespread and beneficial.[6] Nevertheless, it is not as

[2] P. W. Bridgman, "The Nature of Some of Our Physical Concepts," *British Journal for the Philosophy of Science*, VIII (1957), p. 257.

[3] That Einstein employed an operationalist criterion is a controversial thesis. For an argument against this thesis, see Adolf Grunbaum, "Operationism and Relativity," in *The Validation of Scientific Theories*, ed. Phillip G. Frank (New York: Collier Books, 1961).

[4] Thus, B. F. Skinner writes: "In spite of the difference which Stevens pretends to find, behaviorism has been (at least to most behaviorists) nothing more than a thoroughgoing operational analysis of traditional mentalistic concepts." "The Operational Analysis of Psychological Terms," *Psychological Review*, LII (1945), p. 270.

[5] For example, an author of a recent work on linguistics begins his discussion as follows: "1.0 In order to qualify as adequate a linguistic theory must satisfy two sets of different but equally important conditions. 1.1 First it must employ concepts that are operationally definable in terms of empirical techniques. This criterion yields a criterion of the *operational adequacy* of the theory. It needs no justification for it is widely accepted by linguists. We must reject any theory of semantics the terms of which neither refer to observables nor are reducible to observables." (Italics added) John Lyons, *Structural Semantics* (Oxford: Basil Blackwell, 1963), p. 1.

[6] Many would probably agree, for instance, with Hempel's assessment that "the emphasis on 'operational meaning' in scientifically significant discourse has unquestionably afforded a salutary critique of certain types of procedure in philosophy and in empirical science and has provided a strong stimulus for methodological thinking." Carl Hempel, "A Logical Appraisal of Operationism," in Frank, *Validation of Scientific Theories*, p. 58.

apparent that operationalism has succeeded in providing an adequate criterion of meaninglessness. I think it fair to say, in fact, that insofar as operationalism purports to provide such a criterion, it fails completely.

2

The basic reason for operationalism's failure is its inability to explain —in a way that is neither overly restrictive nor largely trivial—just what an operational definition should be. This defect cuts into the core of the proposed criterion. For until we know how to understand the phrase "operationally defined," we will not know how to apply the criterion, nor how to separate the meaningless from the meaningful by appealing to it.

Many of the proponents of operationalism would explain "operational definition" somewhat as follows: an operational definition states that a concept or term is to apply to a particular case if and only if certain *instrumental procedures* are employed. For example, the term "harder than" might be operationally defined by the rule: a piece of mineral, X, is to be called harder than another piece of mineral, Y, if and only if the operation of drawing a sharp point of X across the surface of Y results in a scratch on the latter.[7] So, too, the concept of *average intelligence* might be operationally defined by saying (roughly) that a man is of average intelligence if and only if he scores between 90 and 110 on a particular intelligence test, if he takes the test.

In the above explanation, stress is placed on the phrase "instrumental procedures." Indeed, the linking of a concept to instrumental procedures, rather than to something else, is often taken to be what distinguishes operational definitions and definitions of other types. This linkage, moreover, is supposed to make operational definitions particularly useful for the experimental scientist. It is more important to notice, however, that stressing instrumental procedures makes it reasonably clear what an operational definition should consist of. Some difficulties, however, remain. For example: are the instrumental operations to be operations that have already been performed, as Bridgman has continually insisted—or is it enough that

[7] This illustration and the above explanation, though slightly modified, is borrowed from *ibid.*, p. 56.

the operations could be performed? More liberally still, is it sufficient that we *know* of such instrumental procedures, even if it is technologically impossible, at least for the present, to carry them through? Further, what is to count as the *same* instrumental procedure? That must be determined if we are to know when we are applying identical concepts. For example, the pressure of a gas can be measured by a U-tube manometer and also by an ionization gauge.[8] Since the instrumental procedures that would figure in the operational definition of "gas pressure" are different, are there two concepts of "gas pressure"? Bridgman has continually insisted, in fact, that where the instrumental procedures are different, the concepts are different.[9] If we agree with Bridgman—and agreement on this point raises new difficulties[10]—we still need to explain *how* different the operations may be while defining *one* concept. For example, suppose we define the expression "average intelligence" in terms of scoring in a certain percentile range on a particular intelligence test. Does the use of another test which closely resembles the original test generate a second, distinct concept of average intelligence? If so, what results if we use the same test but change some of the test questions, or translate the test questions into a different language, say Spanish or Italian? The extremes to which psychologists who agreed with Bridgman actually did go are pointed out by Gustav Bergmann: ". . . some refused, presumably on operationist principles, to 'generalize' from one instance of an experiment to the next if the appartatus had in the meantime been moved to another corner of the room."[11] Moreover, the extreme to which we logically *could* go, even if no operationalist has actually done so, is to rule that one and the same concept must be linked to instrumental procedures actually carried out on one and only one occasion. To avoid such a result, which would be intolerably detrimental to the demand for scientific concepts that apply to a wide range of experimental

[8] This illustration is discussed by R. B. Lindsay, "A Critique of Operationalism in Physics," *Philosophy of Science*, IV (1937), p. 458.

[9] For a comparatively recent reaffirmation of this requirement, see P. W. Bridgman's "The Operational Aspect of Meaning" (1950), reprinted in his *Reflections of a Physicist* (New York: Philosophical Library, 1955), p. 126.

[10] See Lindsay on this point, "Critique of Operationalism," p. 458.

[11] Gustav Bergmann, "Sense and Nonsense in Operationalism," in Frank, *Validation of Scientific Theories*, p. 53.

findings, we would have to provide some way of answering the questions asked above. Merely explaining "operational definition" in terms of "instrumental procedure," without attempting to answer such questions, obviously would be insufficient.

The above explanation, nevertheless, does make it reasonably clear how we are to understand the phrase "operational definition." For by stressing the need to link concepts to instrumental procedures the above explanation does indicate what kinds of definitions would and would not qualify as "operational." For example, Newton's definition of "absolute time"—"that which flows by itself uniformly and equably"—would presumably fail to qualify as an operational definition because it makes no mention of any instrumental procedures. If Newton's definition were the only definition of "absolute time" available, therefore, we could use Bridgman's criterion to rule that the expression is meaningless. Moreover, it is just such an expression that the operationalist would presumably wish to exclude as meaningless. By explaining the concept of an operational definition in terms of "instrumental procedures," then, we will have made a reasonably good start in trying to understand how the operationalist criterion is to be applied—although, admittedly, certain questions, such as those I raised earlier, will eventually have to be answered if the criterion is to prove satisfactory.

Although the above explanation helps us to advance in one direction, it seriously retards us in another. It would help us to understand how to apply the operationalist criterion but would do so only at the cost of rendering the criterion intolerably restrictive. For if, in constructing an operational definition, we must link the concept to be defined to instrumental procedures, we will be unable to define operationally some concepts which most scientists, including operationalists, would consider meaningful. Hence, some ostensibly meaningful concepts would have to be adjudged meaningless. Presumably that would be unacceptable even to the operationalist. Moreover, some meaningful concepts which are not definable in terms of instrumental procedures are employed in physics, the very science from which Bridgman claims to have extracted his criterion. One such concept is the concept of an electron; others are the concept of a potential energy function as used in classical mechanics and the concept of a state function as used in quantum mechanics.[12] Bridgman, in fact, is well aware that there are concepts which cannot be defined in terms of instrumental procedures, even if many other operationalists are not. Thus, he writes:

> Now at one time or another some physicists have expressed the idea that all pencil and paper operations are eventually reducible to instrumental operations. It seems to me that there is no acceptable argument as to why this should be necessary or desirable, and I believe that observation shows that theoretical physicists do profitably employ concepts which can in no way be reduced to instrumental operations. Quantum mechanics is full of examples; the psi function is one of the simplest.[13]

3

Because it would be much too restrictive to insist that all concepts be defined in terms of instrumental procedures, Bridgman has allowed that some operational definitions might consist of what he has termed "mental," "verbal," or "paper and pencil" operations. In fact, he made this concession in his original essay, although the point was often ignored by subsequent operationalists. As a result, however, Bridgman has so liberalized his criterion that it is almost wholly trivial. By allowing operational definitions to consist of merely "verbal" (or "pencil and paper") operations, we would seem to allow that any concept whatsoever, no matter how metaphysical, can be operationally defined; and if that is so, then wielding the operationalist criterion will not enable us to strike down as meaningless very many, if any, of the concepts which operationalism was designed to eliminate. Even a concept such as Newton's "absolute time" can be operationally defined if we tolerate operational definitions consisting of so-called verbal operations. We can now offer as an operational definition of his concept the very definition which Newton himself suggested: absolute time is that which flows by itself uniformly and equably. Thus, even the concept of absolute time, the very first concept that Bridgman declared to be

---

[12] On this point, see Lindsay, "Critique of Operationalism," p. 459; and Henry Margenau, "Interpretations and Misinterpretations of Operationalism," in Frank, *Validation of Scientific Theories*, p. 45.

[13] P. W. Bridgman, "Some Implications of Recent Viewpoints in Physics," in Bridgman, *Reflections of a Physicist*, p. 90.

meaningless in his original work,[14] will now qualify as a meaningful concept. Moreover, Bridgman himself has conceded the point. Thus, in a recent essay he writes:

> As I see it there is in the general point of view nothing normative whatever. An operational analysis is always possible, that is, an analysis, into what was done or what happened. An operational analysis can be given of the most obscurely metaphysical definition, such as Newton's definition of absolute time as that which flows by itself uniformly and equably.[15]

I think, then, that operationalism, whatever merits it may have had as a stimulus to methodological reform, may be fairly said to be a failure insofar as it purports to provide an adequate criterion of meaninglessness. The basic reason for this failure, as I have tried to indicate, has been its inability to explain adequately, without impairing the usefulness of the operationalist criterion, what an "operational definition" should consist of. On the one hand, explaining "operational definition" in terms of "instrumental procedures" has made the criterion overly restrictive; while on the other, explaining the concept in terms of verbal as well as instrumental procedures, as Bridgman does, has made it too broad to be of any use. Bridgman, it is true, has suggested a possible way of avoiding this latter result by indicating that we might try to distinguish "good" and "bad" verbal operations. If we were able to do that, perhaps we could still rule out as meaningless concepts that can be operationally defined only through "verbal procedures," such as the concept of absolute time, on the grounds that the operational definitions of such concepts are unacceptable because the constituent operations are "bad." Bridgman has been unable, however, to provide any clear criterion for distinguishing "good" operations from "bad" operations; hence, his suggestion has not provided any adequate means of avoiding a criterion too liberal to be of any use.

The inability of the operationalist to explain what is meant by "operational definition" is by itself a defect fatal to the operationalist program;

[14] See Bridgman, *Logic of Modern Physics*, chapter 1.
[15] Bridgman, *Reflections of a Physicist*, p. 163.

but there are other defects equally decisive. I shall now consider two of them.

4

It is, or at least should have been, obvious that to ask that *all* concepts be operationally defined is to ask too much. There is surely no need to meet such a demand. If there were, almost all that Bridgman has written on operationalism would be nonsense. Even in *The Logic of Modern Physics,* Bridgman provided at most only a few operational definitions; most of the concepts he employed in that work were not defined at all. Thus, if it were true that we do not know the meaning of a concept until it has been operationally defined, we and Bridgman would fail to understand most, if not all, of what was said in *The Logic of Modern Physics.* But Bridgman's work *was* understood, as is shown by the great influence it enjoyed; therefore, it is not true that to be intelligible, every concept must be operationally defined.

It might be replied that Bridgman's work was not really intelligible: people thought they comprehended what was being said, but they were mistaken. The reply, however, overlooks the fact that almost everything that has ever been written—by Bridgman or by anyone else—involves concepts that have not been operationally defined. Thus, either we commit ourselves to the fantastic assertion that nothing (or almost nothing) that has ever been written has been understood by anyone, or we abandon the claim that a concept can be understood only if it has been operationally defined.

Moreover, not only is there no need to define all (meaningful) concepts operationally, there is also no possibility of doing so. It would be impossible to define—either operationally or in any other manner—*every* (meaningful) concept that we employ because in defining a concept X, we must use one or more other concepts, say Y and Z. If every concept needs to be operationally defined before it can be understood, then the concepts Y and Z will not be intelligible until they, too, are operationally defined; and if Y and Z are unintelligible, the definition of X in terms of Y and Z will also be unintelligible. Hence, until Y and Z are defined, we will not understand X, even after it has been defined in terms of Y and Z. We might, of course, try to define Y and Z, but then the problem begins anew: in defining Y and Z, we introduce new concepts which, in turn, will be meaningless until they are operationally defined. It might be thought that the problem could be solved by ultimately making our definitions circular. For example, after defining X in terms of Y and Z, and Y and Z in terms of A, we might then define A in terms of the original concept, X. We would still be unable to understand X, however, since X has not yet been operationally defined in terms of concepts we do understand; hence, defining A in terms of X would be futile. In general, then, if every concept must be operationally defined in order to be understood, no concept whatsoever will be understandable.

In a symposium on operationalism, Professor E. G. Boring asked a question based on an objection similar to the one I have raised. Professor Boring's answer to his own question is worth considering:

> Since the operational definition introduces new conceptual terms, a regress is begun, one which may be infinite. This regress is not, however, embarrassing, for it can be terminated as soon as there is mutual understanding between the speaker and the hearer, as soon as there is no further demand for definition.[16]

The answer, however, is obviously unacceptable *if* we insist that *all* concepts be defined operationally. If we do so insist, we shall never reach a point at which "there is no further demand for definition," for all concepts employed in our definition will need to be defined if they are to be understood. To relax the original demand and insist merely that some concepts be operationally defined raises the new problem of how we distinguish between those (meaningful) concepts that need to be operationally defined and those that do not. To make that distinction, we would need to develop an additional criterion—and that has not been done.

5

The requirement that *all* meaningful concepts must be operationally defined cannot be met. An objection might be made against even a less

---

[16] E. G. Boring, "The Use of Operational Definitions in Science," *Psychological Review*, LII (1945), p. 243.

rigid requirement that most but not all (meaningful) concepts be operationally defined. The objection would not merely be that *certain* meaningful concepts, such as those concepts from physics which I cited earlier, cannot be so defined, but rather that *many,* perhaps most, of the concepts used by scientists and nonscientists alike will resist endlessly our attempts to define them operationally. Take, for example, the concept of average intelligence. I said earlier that this concept might be operationally defined as follows: "A man is of average intelligence if and only if he scores between 90 and 110 on a particular intelligence test, say the Wechsler-Bellevue Intelligence Test, if he takes the test." Such a definition, however, would be quite inadequate. A man might very well be of average intelligence and yet score much *higher* than 110 on the Wechsler-Bellevue Test if, for example, he had learned of the correct answers before taking the test. So, too, a man of average intelligence might score much *lower* than 90 on the same test if he were to break the point of his pencil before finishing the test. It might be objected here that such cases do not show that our original definition is hopelessly inadequate, but rather that it has been stated too crudely. A less crude formulation would contain a clause ruling out such disturbing conditions as "having prior access to the test answers" or "having one's pencil broken." Although this objection is worth making, however, it fails to be adequate because there are an indefinite number of such disturbing conditions; hence, it would be quite difficult, if not impossible, to add a clause to our original definition that would list all such conditions. We might add a clause listing the two conditions I described above, but there would always be other such conditions which, if present, would make the definition inapplicable. For example, the definition might fail to apply if a man of average intelligence were to take the test while in great physical pain, or after not having slept for three nights, or while being threatened by the examiner, etc. Here it might be answered that there is no need to attempt to list all of what amounts to an indefinitely large number of such conditions. Instead, we might simply append the phrase "all other things being equal." Thus, the definition would read: "A man is of average intelligence if and only if he scores between 90 and 110 on the Wechsler-Bellevue Test, if he takes the test, all other things being equal." The emendation, however, defeats the very purpose of operationalism; for how can the phrase "all other things being equal" be defined operationally? The dilemma then is this: either we cannot define a concept such as average intelligence operationally (because we cannot list all of the indefinitely large number of disturbing conditions), or we can define the concept only with the aid of a second concept which is not of an operational character.[17]

If this last objection is sound, and if, as I am claiming, such an objection could be used to defeat attempts to define operationally many, perhaps most, of the concepts used by both scientists and nonscientists, we should expect to find that few concepts have ever been given operational definitions. How could that be? It might not be surprising if most "non-scientific" concepts have never been operationally defined, but what of the concepts employed in, say, psychology—the field in which operationalism is said to have had such a great impact? The fact is that very few psychological concepts have been operationally defined. If we look at the works of the leading operationalists in psychology—for example, the works of Clark L. Hull, B. F. Skinner, S. S. Stevens, E. G. Boring, and H. Eysenck—we will find few instances of operational definitions. Furthermore, there is no incompatibility between asserting that operationalism was influential in psychology while conceding that few operational definitions were ever constructed. The reason is that as applied by psychologists (and other social scientists), operationalism was transformed into the thesis that to be scientifically acceptable a statement must be empirically testable. Moreover, even this thesis was thought by many to be too narrow and was subsequently broadened: rather than requiring that every statement of a theory be testable, it was merely insisted that the theory as a whole be testable.[18] Evidence seems to show that the insistence that all theories be

[17] This kind of objection was first pointed out to me by Peter Achinstein. A similar objection is made by Rudolf Carnap, "The Methodological Character of Theoretical Concepts," in *Foundations of Science and the Concepts of Psychology and Psychoanalysis,* eds. Herbert Feigl and Michael Scriven ("Minnesota Studies in the Philosophy of Science," vol. 1; Minneapolis: University of Minnesota Press, 1956), pp. 108–9.

[18] For example, the psychologist Albert Ellis gives the following characterization of operationalism: "To be operationally meaningful, a statement must be confirmable at least in principle: that is to say, a scientific theory must be tied to observables at some point. It may be part of a whole network of other statements or theories; but eventually, somewhere along the line it must be related to observables." Albert Ellis, "An Operational Reformulation of Some of the Basic Principles of Psychoanalysis," in *Foundations of Science,* eds. Feigl and Scriven, p. 132.

testable has been of great significance in stimulating methodological reform in psychology. In that sense operationalism did have a great impact. But there is no reason why this demand for testability should necessarily generate an abundance of operational definitions, for testability and definability are not the same. It may be quite *reasonable* to demand that a theory be testable—that is, be linked in some way to experience—and yet it may be quite *unreasonable* to require that every concept in every statement of the theory be rigorously defined, operationally or any other way. If there is no *a priori* reason for the operationalist movement to produce operational definitions, I think the evidence will show—although I have not tried to present such evidence here—that very few such definitions, in fact, were ever constructed.

6

I should conclude with a brief disclaimer. Nothing that I have said above is intended as an attack on the requirement that a scientific theory taken as a whole must be testable. It is difficult to quarrel with such a requirement. Nor have I disputed what might be called "the weak thesis" of operationalism: that it is useful to try to link individual scientific concepts in some way—although not necessarily in as rigid a way as explicit definition—to instrumental procedures. Whether this weaker thesis is acceptable, it seems to me, can be decided best by those actively engaged in scientific research. At any rate, I have taken no stand on the issue. What I have tried to argue, instead, is that operationalism is a failure *insofar as* it purports to provide an adequate criterion of meaninglessness. It is a failure on this one point, to sum up what I have been arguing, for the following reasons:

1. It has proved impossible to explain what an "operational definition" is without making the criterion either too liberal or too restrictive.

2. It is too demanding to ask that *all* concepts be operationally defined: such a requirement need not be met and could not be met. If not all concepts need be operationally defined, we would need some further criterion to tell us which concepts are exempt from the requirement.

3. Finally, most concepts employed by scientists and nonscientists

cannot be operationally defined without the aid of some such phrase as: "all other things being equal." But the insertion of such a phrase in an operational definition would be compatible with operationalism only if the phrase, in turn, could be operationally defined; but it is difficult to see how that could be done.

chapter ii

verificationism

The verifiability criterion was said to have been first employed by Albert Einstein. Morris Schlick, for example, said that in advocating the use of the verifiability criterion, he was only "following Einstein."[1] Moreover, Hans Reichenbach has argued that the criterion played a central role in Einstein's development of the Special Theory of Relativity.[2] As I noted earlier, Bridgman made a similar claim about the operationalist criterion; and just as there is some doubt that Bridgman was entitled to invoke Einstein's authority, a similar doubt may be voiced about the verifiability criterion. There is a passage in Einstein's writings—quoted at the beginning of the Introduction—which is often pointed to as proof that Einstein accepted either an operationalist or verifiability criterion. Moreover, the passage does suggest a commitment to both criteria, even if it does not establish conclusively that this was Einstein's view. The passage was written, however, in 1916—eleven years after the publication of the original paper on the special theory—and would show at most that Einstein accepted a verifiability criterion in 1916, not that he employed such a criterion in formulating the Special Theory of Relativity. Moreover, I think that a study of Einstein's original paper of 1905 will fail to produce a single

[1] For example, Schlick writes: "All I am trying to do is to stick consistently to Einstein's position and to admit no exceptions from it," in "Meaning and Verification," *Philosophical Review*, XLV (1936), p. 343.

[2] See Hans Reichenbach, "The Philosophical Significance of the Theory of Relativity" in *Albert Einstein: Philosopher-Scientist*, ed. Paul Schilpp (Evanston, Illinois: The Library of Living Philosophers, 1949).

passage suggesting that he was employing a meaning criterion of any kind. Einstein did, it is true, refuse to postulate the existence of a "luminiferous ether." But he did not refuse to do so, as Reichenbach suggests, on the grounds that such a postulation would be meaningless because the Michelson experiment had failed to verify such an assertion. Einstein is quite clear on this point. He refrained from asserting the existence of an ether simply because, given the Special Theory of Relativity, there was no need to do so. "The introduction of a 'luminiferous ether,' " he writes,

will prove to be superfluous inasmuch as the view here to be developed will not require an 'absolutely stationary space' provided with special properties, nor assign a velocity-vector to a point of the empty space in which electromagnetic processes take place.[3]

An amusing footnote to the controversy about whether Einstein accepted either an operationalist or verifiability criterion is provided by Phillip Frank in his biography of Einstein. In discussing Bohr's positivistic interpretation of quantum mechanics, Einstein is quoted as saying:

A new fashion has now arisen in physics. By means of ingeniously formulated theoretical experiments it is proved that certain physical magnitudes cannot be measured, or, to put it more precisely, that according to accepted natural laws the investigated bodies behave in such a way as to baffle all attempts at measurement. From this the conclusion is drawn that it is completely meaningless to retain these magnitudes in the language of physics. To speak about them is pure metaphysics.

To this, Frank replied: "But the fashion you speak of was invented by you in 1905?" Einstein answered: "A good joke should not be repeated too often."[4]

The positivists did not credit Einstein as the sole source of the verifiability criterion; they also acknowledged their indebtedness to Witt-

[3] Albert Einstein, "On the Electrodynamics of Moving Bodies" (1905), reprinted in *The Principle of Relativity,* eds. Albert Einstein and others (New York: Dover Publications, 1923), p. 38.
[4] Phillip Frank, *Einstein: His Life and Times* (New York: Alfred A. Knopf, 1953), p. 216.

20

genstein. But here, too, their crediting is questionable. For one thing, no statement of the criterion can be found in Wittgenstein's *Tractatus Logico-Philosophicus,* the work which is said to have exerted a major influence on the positivist movement. The absence of a statement in itself would certainly not be decisive, for Wittgenstein influenced the positivists in his personal conversations as well as in his writings.[5] Moreover, there is direct evidence—in the lecture notes of Professor Alice Ambrose—that at least in his lectures of 1932–33, Wittgenstein suggested a commitment to what appears to be a version of the verifiability criterion. He is quoted as saying: "In the verification of a proposition lies its sense. . . . If we do away with all means of verification we destroy the meaning."[6] What is questionable is whether the positivists, and others, have understood his suggestions. There is some evidence that they did not. Thus, Wittgenstein is reported to have remarked:

I used at one time to say that in order to get clear how a certain sentence is used, it was a good idea to ask oneself the question: How would one try to verify such an assertion? But that's just one way of getting clear about the use of a word or sentence. . . . Some people have turned this suggestion about asking for the verification into a dogma—as if I'd been advancing a *theory* about meaning.[7]

I think the above at least renders questionable the assertion that either Einstein or Wittgenstein employed a verifiability criterion, although I am not arguing that such an assertion is without any foundation at all. What I am arguing is that the evidence is inconclusive; however, the question of origins, although of some interest to the historian, need not be settled here. What primarily concerns me is the adequacy of the verifiability criterion, and, on this point, it matters little whether the criterion was first used by Einstein, Wittgenstein, or the village dullard.

[5] For example, Schlick writes: "If the preceding remarks about meaning are as correct as I am convinced they are, this will, to a large measure, be due to conversations with Wittgenstein which have greatly influenced my own views about these matters." Schlick, "Meaning and Verification," p. 341.

[6] Alice Ambrose, "Metamorphoses of the Principle of Verifiability," in *Current Philosophical Issues,* ed. F. C. Dommeyer (Springfield, Illinois: Charles C. Thomas, 1966), p. 68.

[7] Quoted by John Passmore in *A Hundred Years of Philosophy* (London: Gerald Duckworth and Co. Ltd., 1957), p. 371.

1

From the beginning, the career of the verifiability criterion suffered the same fluctuations as the operationalist criterion. At first, a model of the criterion was promoted that was strong enough to do away with most unwanted metaphysical statements. It was shortly discovered, as it was with the operationalist criterion, that the results were too sweeping: not only metaphysics, but much of science as well, would succumb to such a criterion. Hence, the first model was dropped, and a new, weaker version was marketed. The results, however, were unsatisfactory for a different reason: instead of being too powerful, the new version proved to be too weak to eliminate most of the ostensibly meaningless statements. All subsequent versions of the criterion have met the same fate: either they have been so destructive that they obliterated much that was surely meaningful, or they have been so feeble that they were unable to eliminate even obviously meaningless statements. The history of these unsuccessful attempts to formulate the criterion adequately has been so well documented by a number of writers[8] that my re-telling the story in any detail here would be superfluous. It might be useful, however, to trace a few of the most well-known efforts at stating the criterion and to show how they failed.

One difference between the verifiability criterion and the operationalist criterion is that the former was applicable to whole sentences or statements,[9] while the latter was applied to individual concepts or terms.[10] The statements to be covered by the verifiability criterion, moreover, were all empirical (as opposed to being analytic); hence, in what follows, it should be understood that I am referring only to empirical statements, even if that is not explicitly stated. Further, the positivists stressed (at least in their recent writings) that they were speaking only of "cognitive" meaning, as opposed to "poetic" or "emotive" meaning, when they asserted that

[8] For particularly good accounts, see Carl Hempel, "Problems and Changes in the Empiricist Criterion of Meaning," in *Semantics and the Philosophy of Language,* ed. Leonard Linsky (Urbana, Illinois: The University of Illinois Press, 1952), and Israel Scheffler, *The Anatomy of Inquiry* (New York: Alfred A. Knopf, 1963).

[9] I am using "sentence" and "statement" interchangeably here; later (in chapter IV), I shall distinguish the two.

[10] Carnap's latest formulation of the verifiability criterion, however, also applies to terms.

certain statements lacked meaning. Since, however, the positivists used "cognitively meaningless" in the same way that I am using "meaningless" (tentatively, to mean "neither true nor false"), I shall omit the qualifier "cognitive" and speak simply of *meaningless* statements.

One of the earliest formulations of the criterion stressed complete verifiability. As Hempel has expressed it: a sentence has empirical meaning if and only if it is not analytic and follows logically from some finite and logically consistent class of observation-sentences.[11] This formulation, however, was soon discovered to be too strong. For given such a requirement, statements of universal form—such as "All bodies fall at a constant rate of speed"—would be meaningless because they are not conclusively verifiable even in principle by any finite set of observational data. Requiring complete falsifiability, instead of complete verifiability, seemed to be too demanding for a similar reason. Although universal statements could be completely falsified, existential statements—such as "There exists at least one unicorn" —could not, or at least so it was thought. Further, there are other sentences, containing so-called mixed quantifiers, which could be neither verified nor falsified conclusively. For example, the statement "For any substance there exists some solvent" seems to be meaningful but was thought to be neither completely verifiable nor completely falsifiable. For these reasons, and others, requirements of complete verifiability and complete falsifiability were abandoned in favor of a weaker requirement. Instead of demanding that a statement be completely verifiable (or falsifiable), it was merely required that all meaningful empirical statements be capable of being confirmed or disconfirmed to some degree. Various criteria were then set up to indicate when a statement was confirmable. For example, Ayer devised a criterion according to which a statement is confirmable, and hence meaningful, if it is possible to derive from the statement and its subsidiary hypotheses an observation-statement not derivable from the subsidiary hypotheses alone. It was soon discovered, however, that his criterion would allow almost any statement whatsoever to be significant. For example, from "The absolute is perfect" and "If the absolute is perfect, then this apple is red," one can deduce "This apple is

---

[11] See Hempel, "The Empiricist Criterion of Meaning," p. 45.

red"—a deduction which does not follow from the first statement alone.[12]

Since Ayer recognized the defect of his formulation, he presented a new version in the introduction to the second edition of his *Language, Truth and Logic*. Under the new formulation, the subsidiary hypotheses were required to be either analytic or independently testable in the sense of the modified criterion.[13] This new criterion, however, was shown to be too liberal to be of any use. Thus, Professor A. Church, in his review of Ayer's book in the *Journal of Symbolic Logic*, showed that if there are at least three observation-statements, none of which entails any of the others, then it follows for any statement whatever that either it or its denial would be significant, according to Ayer's revised criterion.[14]

One additional formulation of the verifiability criterion should be mentioned. In 1956, Carnap proposed a new version which would be applicable to terms rather than to sentences, a much more modest proposal than those discussed earlier. Even if Carnap's new criterion were successful in enabling us to decide which terms could appear in meaningful statements, however, it would still not enable us to rule against nonsensical statements composed only of meaningful terms. The criterion would be useless in evaluating such statements as "Saturday is in bed," statements which have been referred to as "category mistakes."[15] Moreover, even measured in terms of its more modest aspirations, Carnap's latest criterion has been shown to be defective.[16]

Further difficulties arise in various other versions of the verifiability criterion. For example, most writers have tried to explain "confirmation" in terms of "deducibility." Thus, Ayer wrote in both of his formulations of deducing observation statements from the statement being evaluated. But

---

[12] I am closely following Hempel here; see his discussion, *ibid.*, p. 49.

[13] A. J. Ayer, *Language, Truth and Logic* (2d ed.; London: Gollancz, 1946), p. 13.

[14] A. Church, Review of Ayer, *Language, Truth and Logic*, in *The Journal of Symbolic Logic* (1949), pp. 52–53.

[15] This point is made by G. Schlesinger in "Terms and Sentences of Empirical Science," *Mind*, LXXIII (1964), p. 400.

[16] For relevant criticisms see: S. F. Barker, *Induction and Hypothesis* (Ithaca, New York: Cornell University Press, 1957), pp. 136–42; Edward H. Madden and Murray J. Kiteley, "Postulates and Meaning," *Philosophy of Science*, XXIX (1962); and Peter Achinstein, "Theoretical Terms and Partial Interpretation," *British Journal for the Philosophy of Science*, XV (1964).

that seems to beg the question. If only meaningful statements can appear in deductions—as is usually thought—then we would have to *assume* that a statement is meaningful before we could, by deducing observational consequences, *prove* that it is meaningful.[17]

Apart from this problem, a new difficulty has arisen from recent discussions of the alleged distinction between theoretical and observational terms. A number of writers have argued that the notion of an "observational term" (or "observation-statement") is irremediably defective. The criticism is not merely that there are items not happily classifiable as either "observational" or "nonobservational" but rather something more radical: namely, what is said to be observational or nonobservational depends upon the situation in which the observation takes place. Rather than explain the workings of these arguments,[18] I would merely point out the following: if such arguments are sound, and if we insist on explaining "confirmability" in terms of "observational language" or in terms of observation-statements, then it will not be possible to formulate a "context-free" criterion—i.e., a criterion which shows that certain statements are meaningless in *all* situations.

There are other difficulties of a more technical kind, some of which are intimately related to the mechanics of truth-functional logic, which have also plagued all attempts at formulating an adequate criterion.[19] Because of these difficulties, and because of the other problems discussed earlier, most philosophers today, I think, would agree that the task of formulating an adequate verifiability or confirmability criterion is hopeless. For the most part, the task has been abandoned. Not *all* philosophers, of course, would agree with this pessimism; some believe that, despite the past failures, an effective criterion may some day be worked out.[20] Nevertheless, as of today, after thirty or forty years of use of the concept of meaningless-

[17] For an attempt to circumvent this difficulty, see Wesley C. Salmon, "Verifiability and Logic," in *Mind, Matter and Method,* eds. Paul K. Feyerabend and Grover Maxwell (Minneapolis: University of Minnesota Press, 1966), pp. 359–62.

[18] The relevant arguments can be found in Fred Dretske, "Observational Terms," *Philosophical Review,* LXXIII (1964), and Peter Achinstein, "The Problem of Theoretical Terms," *American Philosophical Quarterly,* II (1965).

[19] Some of these technical difficulties are discussed by Salmon, "Verifiability and Logic."

[20] For example, Feigl, Carnap, and Salmon presumably still share this belief.

ness, we still have no adequate, general criterion for proving that a statement is meaningless.[21]

2

Thus far I have tacitly conceded that an adequate verifiability criterion may yet be worked out, even though all past attempts have failed. I shall now argue that very probably an adequate criterion will not be worked out. Three arguments may be advanced to support that contention.

My first argument concerns the feasibility of devising a criterion that can be easily *applied*. Let us assume that the criterion can be stated in such a way that it will neither exclude any statements that are clearly meaningful, nor sanction any statements that are clearly meaningless. Most proponents of verificationism now agree that, insofar as there is hope of adequately stating the criterion at all, such a formulation would have to be in terms of confirmability in principle. By confirmability in principle is meant the logical possibility that some conceivable observations be relevant to either the confirmation or disconfirmation of the statement being evaluated.[22] If that is all that is required, then it will prove very difficult to apply such a criterion. How is it to be shown that it is *logically impossible* to confirm (or disconfirm) any given statement? Take, for example, the often-used illustration of a meaningless statement, "The Absolute is perfect." It may be that this statement is in no way confirmable. It may be, in fact, that it is *in principle* impossible to confirm this statement, but that is not so obvious. It is not obviously self-contradictory, for example, to assert that the statement "The Absolute is perfect" has been confirmed to some degree. If it is not obvious, however, that this statement cannot, in principle, be confirmed, then how do we go about demonstrating that it cannot? It is not enough merely to point out that we do not *know* of any way to

---

[21] I have so far discussed only the operationalist and verifiability criteria; for a critique of the category or type criterion, see chapter III.

[22] Carnap, for example, states his "Principle of Confirmability": "If it is in principle impossible for any conceivable observational result to be either confirming or disconfirming evidence for a linguistic expression A, then expression A is devoid of cognitive meaning." Paul Schilpp, ed., *The Philosophy of Rudolf Carnap* (LaSalle, Illinois: Open Court, 1963), p. 874.

confirm the statement, for the same might be true of obviously meaningful statements. It must be *shown* that it is logically impossible to confirm the statement; and this, in general, is a very difficult thing to do. This is not to say that no statement whatsoever could be shown to be meaningless by use of the criterion, but what this does suggest is that it would be very difficult to apply such a criterion in many cases.

It might be thought that this difficulty can be met by insisting, as Salmon does (following Reichenbach), that it be *physically possible*—instead of merely logically possible—to verify the statement in question. The illustration of physical impossibility which Salmon cites is taken from quantum physics. His point, presumably, is this: it is an implication of quantum theory that an assertion that a particle has a determinate position and velocity is unverifiable. Hence, if quantum theory is true, then—necessarily—we cannot verify such a statement. Nevertheless, such a statement is not unverifiable in principle, for quantum theory might be false. Rather, the statement is, according to Salmon, "physically" unverifiable. This kind of unverifiability, however, is to be distinguished from mere "technological" unverifiability—which, according to Salmon, can be overcome "by increased knowledge and improved technology."[23] It had once been technically impossible to photograph the far side of the moon, for example, but it had never been physically impossible.

Even if Salmon's proposal is not overly restrictive, as most positivists have thought, to insist on the physical possibility of verification will not appreciably help matters because it is comparatively rare to have a well-confirmed theory which tells us, as quantum theory does, that if the theory is true, then a certain statement is unverifiable. The most we are likely to be able to say is that a *particular* way of verifying a given statement is physically impossible, not that *all conceivable ways* of verifying such a statement are physically impossible. For example, it may be physically impossible to verify an assertion about the density of matter on a particular star in the Andromeda galaxy by actually visiting the star, since the galaxy is approximately 1,500,000 light years away. Moreover, this physical impossibility can be shown by appealing to evidence from both biology

[23] Salmon, "Verifiability and Logic," p. 371.

(concerning the probable life-span of a human organism) and relativity theory (concerning the upper bound of space travel velocity). That *one* means of verification is physically impossible, however, does not obviate the possibility that some other way of verifying the statement—for example, by the use of radio astronomy—might be feasible. Moreover, Salmon's proposal would seem to be of little help in evaluating the statement I cited earlier. It may be that it is physically impossible to verify "The Absolute is perfect," but it is difficult to see how that could be shown.

This first objection is not meant to be decisive. I am merely arguing that even if the verifiability criterion could be stated so as to be neither too restrictive nor too liberal, that would not mean that the criterion could be satisfactorily applied. To apply the criterion easily, some means would have to be devised for showing that a statement were not verifiable (or confirmable); without such an additional aid, the problem of proving "meaninglessness" would be merely shifted to that of proving "unverifiability."

The second, and more crucial objection is simply this: even if we could state the verifiability criterion in a way that was neither too liberal nor too restrictive, the criterion would still be useless. Moreover, that would be true even if we could very readily apply the criterion, i.e., even if we could easily prove the impossibility of verification. Suppose that for any statement, S, it could be shown that S could not possibly be verified (or confirmed) in the manner required by the criterion. How would that help in proving S meaningless? It would *not* help, unless we could show that unverifiability (or uncomfirmability) made it necessary, or at least probable, that a statement be meaningless. But this has never been shown, and I doubt, for the following reason, that it could be shown.

We could prove that lack of verifiability implied lack of meaning *if* we could demonstrate that "meaningless" meant, at least in part, "unverifiable." But it is difficult to see how we could establish *that*. It is not *obviously* self-contradictory to assert that some meaningful statements are unverifiable (or even unconfirmable to any extent). Although the fact that something is not obviously self-contradictory does *not* mean that there is no hidden contradiction, it does make it imperative that the verificationist prove, if that be his contention, that "meaningless" means "unverifiable." I doubt that it could be proved. Until it is, a verifiability criterion, even an otherwise adequate one, will be useless in proving "meaninglessness." The original problem of proving that certain statements are meaningless will merely be replaced by another: that of proving that unverifiable statements are meaningless. In shifting the problem, the gain would be nothing.

It might be objected that I am asking too much in demanding a proof that "meaningless" means (in part) "unverifiable." All that needs to be shown, it might be said, is that lack of verifiability makes it *probable,* not necessary, that a statement is meaningless. For instance, we can show that the whistling of the tea kettle is a reliable indication that the water is boiling, but we do not need to demonstrate that there is a (logically) *necessary* connection between whistling tea kettles and boiling water. All we need to show, instead, is that the water is *probably* boiling if the tea kettle is whistling. So, too, all we need to show is that a statement is probably meaningless if it is unverifiable.

I agree with this objection insofar as it makes the point that establishing a probable connection between unverifiability and meaninglessness would be sufficient, but what the objection ignores is the difficulty in establishing any such inductive connection between unverifiability and meaninglessness. In the case of the tea kettle, we have an *independent* test to tell us whether a probability relationship exists. For example, immediately after the whistle sounds, we can pour the water into a tea cup; if the water bubbles and emits steam, then that is a good indication that it is boiling. In the case of verifiability, however, we have nothing analogous to bubbles and steam; that is, we have no independent way of establishing that a statement is meaningless. It is precisely because we have no independent test, moreover, that the development of a verifiability criterion seemed urgent in the first place.

Of course, in the tea kettle case, we need not use the bubbles and steam test. We could ascertain directly that the water is boiling—say, by dipping our finger into it. If the water were to scald our finger, then we would have sufficient proof that the water was boiling, or at least very hot. Why not do something analogous in the case of verifiability? Instead of looking at controversial statements, statements which we need to *prove* meaningless, why not concentrate only on obviously meaningless statements? As in the case of the boiling water, then, we could ascertain that the property in question was present by direct inspection, thus foregoing the need for an independent test. The positivist and the metaphysician could sit down together and draw up a list containing only those statements which both agree are obviously meaningless. Then the statements could be checked to see if they are unverifiable. If they were, then it might be concluded that there is an inductive relationship between meaninglessness and unverifiability. Unfortunately, however, there are two objections to the above procedure, each of which is lethal. In the first place, both the metaphysician and positivist will agree that if a statement is meaningless— or at least, if it is known to be meaningless—then the statement is unverifiable. Here the positivist and metaphysician will agree that there *is* a necessary connection. The problem is to show that the relation runs in the other direction: that "unverifiability" implies "meaninglessness." Since being meaningless, or being known to be meaningless, implies being unverifiable, then the metaphysician will explain that the meaningless statements on the list are unverifiable *because* they are meaningless. That meaninglessness and unverifiability go together here does not provide evidence that they will always, or even usually, go together: it only provides evidence that a meaningless statement will be unverifiable—and we already knew that. Second, the metaphysician will argue that there is positive evidence that statements are not meaningless because they are unverifiable. The positive evidence is that there are a number of statements, such as "The Absolute is perfect," which are unverifiable and yet are *not* meaningless. The metaphysician, then, will surely not agree that the fact that a statement is unverifiable makes it probable that the statement is meaningless. We might convince him, of course, if we could show that there is a necessary, conceptual connection between being unverifiable and being meaningless; but, once again, no one has ever established that—and I do not see how it could be established.

Here it might be objected that I have not treated the verifiability criterion in the spirit in which the positivists themselves presented it. Ayer, it is true, did assert that in one use of the term "meaning," it would be incorrect—and he meant *necessarily* incorrect—to say that a statement was meaningful even if it did not satisfy the verifiability criterion.[24] But Carnap, Feigl, and others in the positivist tradition refrained from making such a claim, at least in their later writings. Instead they presented the criterion as an "explication"—in Carnap's technical sense of this term—of the concept of meaningfulness (or meaninglessness, depending upon how we state the criterion). Viewed as an "explication," the criterion is to be considered as something being proposed, not as something which should be stated in the form of a proposition. As Feigl writes: "Logical empiricists recognize today that this criterion formulated as a principle is a proposal and not a proposition."[25] When regarding the criterion in this spirit, we can sensibly ask whether it should be adopted or rejected, but we cannot sensibly ask whether it is true or false, since proposals, unlike propositions, are neither true nor false. In deciding whether to accept the proposal, Feigl points out, we can ask two questions. We can ask, first, whether the explication adequately represents the way the term "meaningless" is used in the language of science and common sense. About this, Feigl admits, there is a "great deal of opportunity for dispute."[26] But it is a second question that Feigl thinks is more important: namely, is the proposal a fruitful one? Feigl answers it as follows: "The vindication of the criterion must then consist in showing that its adoption will produce the sort of clarity that we seek when we realize that confusion of the various functions of language leads only to endless perplexity and vexation with pseudo problems. In other words, if we do not wish to open the floodgates to countless questions which by their very construction are in principle unanswerable, then the adoption of the confirmability criterion is indispensable."[27]

Fiegl's attempt to vindicate the adoption of the verifiability criterion, and all similar attempts that I am aware of, are unsuccessful. But that is not very important for my argument. Even if such vindications were successful, they would in no way provide a satisfactory answer to my second objection

[24] Ayer, *Language, Truth and Logic,* pp. 15–16. Ayer makes no attempt to justify his assertion and, in fact, concedes that the metaphysician would not be convinced by his claim.

[25] Herbert Feigl, "De Principiis Non Disputandum," in *Philosophical Analysis,* ed. Max Black (Ithaca, New York: Cornell University Press, 1950), p. 140.

[26] *Ibid.,* p. 141.

[27] *Ibid.*

and are in fact irrelevant to it. I shall now try to justify both of these assertions.

If we ask the two questions which Feigl says are pertinent to the positivist proposal, the answer to each should prove quite discouraging to the verificationist. To the first question, concerning the adequacy of the explication, the answer of the nonverificationist—the person we are trying to convince—must be unfavorable. In the explicated sense of "meaning," propositions which are meaningful but not confirmable will lack meaning; they will be meaningful in the usual sense but will be meaningless in the new, explicated sense. Hence, there is a lack of correspondence between the usual sense of "meaning" and the explicated sense. Of course, we might try to show that the nonverificationist's answer to the first question is mistaken and try to demonstrate that in the ordinary sense of "meaning," as well as in the explicated sense, "meaningful" means (in part) "confirmable." But then we would have no need of a vindication at all, for then we would not be *replacing* the ordinary concept of "meaning"—we would be merely saying what the ordinary concept means.

Feigl concedes, however, that there is "a great deal of opportunity for dispute" concerning this first question; it is the second question which is important to his "vindication." But here the verificationist fares no better. Feigl says that adoption of the confirmability criterion is indispensable for holding closed the floodgates to unanswerable questions. But that is false; and since it is, the attempt at vindication fails. Suppose it were true that by making unconfirmable assertions—for example, that "The Absolute is perfect"—we generate "unanswerable" questions, such as "Does the Absolute exist?", "Is He really perfect?", etc. The confirmability criterion would still not be shown to be indispensable or even useful. We can simply refrain from making such statements. Why, then, should anyone adopt the new explicated sense of "meaning"? The metaphysician has no reason to adopt it. Even if the metaphysician could be convinced both that his metaphysical statements generate unanswerable questions and that it is useful to prevent the generation of such questions, he could more easily achieve this goal by simply refraining from making such statements and advising his fellow metaphysicians to do the same. Following this procedure would be easier than adopting and applying a meaning criterion. Moreover, the verificationist should not adopt the explicated sense of "meaning," for if he wishes to prevent the multiplication of unanswerable questions, he should simply try to convince the metaphysician straight off of the disutility of making such statements. There is no need to do the extra work of first presenting a proposal about the use of the term "meaning" and then of trying to convince others of the utility of adopting the proposal, by convincing them of the disutility of making statements which generate insoluable puzzles. Convince the metaphysician that he should refrain from making unconfirmable statements and the need to adopt the new, explicated sense of "meaning" is destroyed; fail to convince the metaphysician that he should refrain from making unconfirmable statements and the attempted vindication of the explication fails. The attempted vindication is unsuccessful either way.

I said earlier that although Feigl's attempted vindication fails, it would make no difference to my argument if it were successful. I shall now show why.

Suppose that it could be shown that it *is* useful to adopt the positivist's explicated sense of "meaning." Using subscripts to keep our accounts straight, let us designate the explicated sense "meaning$_1$," to distinguish it from the original concept, "meaning." There will then be second, explicated senses of "meaningless" and "meaningful," which can be labeled "meaningless$_1$" and "meaningful$_1$." Now, suppose that because we have been convinced of the utility of the positivist's proposal everyone, including the metaphysician, agrees to use the new, explicated concept. As a result, it would seem to follow that certain statements, by definition of the new concept, are "meaningless"—namely, those that cannot be confirmed or disconfirmed in principle. That assumption, however, would not be valid. What follows from the definition of the new concept, "meaning$_1$," is that unconfirmable statements are "meaningless$_1$," not "meaningless." Thus, we might prove that "The Absolute is perfect" is "meaningless$_1$" if we could show that the statement were, in principle, unconfirmable; we would not be proving, however, that "The Absolute is perfect" is "meaningless." We would, in fact, have made no progress at all in proving that this statement, or any statement like it, is "meaningless." Hence, even if it could be shown that it would be useful to replace our usual concept of "meaningfulness" with a new, related concept according to which the statement of the verifiability criterion is true by definition, that would in no way help to justify claims that certain statements are "meaningless." I think it is clear, then, that even a successful vindication of the positivist proposal would have no effect on my argument. Even if a satisfactory criterion could be worked out, and even if we could devise some technique for readily determining when statements were in principle unconfirmable, our efforts would come to nothing—unless we could show that a statement's unverifiability or unconfirmability made it necessary, or at least probable, that the statement is "meaningless." No one, however, has shown that, and it is difficult to see how it could be shown.

I said earlier that my second objection is more crucial than the first; however, it is still not *absolutely* decisive. It *is* decisive in that *if* we believe that the problem of justifying the use of the verifiability criterion is not likely to be solved, then we should be pessimistic about the future of the criterion—even if we believe that, despite past failures, there is hope of satisfactorily stating the criterion. But the argument is not completely decisive, for we may, contrary to what I am assuming, have reason to believe that the problem of justification is also likely to be solved. Now I would like to present a brief argument to show why the belief about solving the justification problem should be abandoned. This third and final argument, then, should be absolutely decisive if it is sound and should leave no hope for the future of the verificationist program.

The positivists have long since abandoned the insistence on what may be called *direct* verification.[28] As Feigl writes: "The issue as it concerns us here turns on the so called 'weaker verifiability criterion,' i.e., the condition of (at least) incomplete and indirect verifiability or refutability."[29] Although it may not be possible to draw any *one,* general distinction between direct and indirect verification, we can at least draw the distinction in some cases. For example, suppose that someone asserts that the president is now in the White House. We might be able to verify this assertion *directly* by going to the White House and observing that he is there. I could also

[28] That a positivist would wish to distinguish direct and indirect verification was pointed out to me by Stephen F. Barker.
[29] Feigl, "De Principiis," p. 140.

indirectly verify the assertion by telephoning the president's press secretary and checking with him.

It is easy to see why the demand for direct verification had to be abandoned. There are statements that are clearly meaningful, and yet cannot—even in principle—be directly verified. For example, the statement, "Even after the last observer dies, and no further observations are made, the sun will continue to rise in the East," is clearly meaningful. In fact, we have good evidence that the statement is true. But we cannot, in principle, *directly* verify such an assertion. If directly verifying the assertion would be to observe the sun continuing to rise in the East, then it would be self-contradictory to say: "I have observed the sun continuing to rise in the East after the last observer had died and no further observations had been made." There is good reason to believe, then, that "meaningless" does not mean (even in part) "incapable of direct verification." Hence, if we have hopes of stating the criterion *only* in terms of *direct* verification, then there is good reason to believe that we will never succeed in justifying the use of the criterion. If "meaningless" did mean "incapable of direct verification," there could not be any meaningful statements incapable (even in principle) of direct verification. It is clear, however, that there are such statements.

The positivists are aware of this point, and all they are now requiring is that a statement be *indirectly* confirmable. I would now like to show, however, that if we allow that *indirect* confirmation can be sufficient, justification of the criterion becomes pointless. Even if it were possible to demonstrate that "meaningless" means "not indirectly confirmable," the demonstration would be useless, for the criterion whose use would then be justified would apply to nothing. To see that this is so, consider the following.

The class of statements to which a criterion of "meaningless" can be usefully applied cannot include statements that are *known* to be meaningless. If we already know that a given statement is meaningless, instead of merely suspecting that it is, we do not need a criterion to justify our belief. Either our belief is already justified, or we do not know that the statement is meaningless. So, too, the class does not include any statement known to be either true or false. Any statement known to be either true or false is known to be meaningful and hence could not be shown to be meaningless by the use of any criterion. Of course, we might prove to be meaningless a statement that we had thought to be true or had thought to be false; but if we did that, we would only show that we were mistaken in thinking the statement true or false.

The class of statements to which a "not indirectly confirmable" criterion of meaninglessness could be applied, then, would contain only statements not already known to be true, false, or meaningless. The entire class would then be empty, for apart from those statements already known to be either true, false, or meaningless—statements which I shall henceforth ignore—any statement whatsoever can be indirectly confirmed. I shall now show how this is so.

Consider the following remark by Bertrand Russell: "Dr. Godel's most interesting paper on my mathematical logic came into my hands after my reply had been completed, and at a time when I had no leisure to work on it. As it is now about eighteen years since I last worked on mathematical logic, it would have taken me a long time to form a critical estimate of Dr. Godel's opinions. His great ability, as shown in his previous work, makes me think it highly probable that many of his criticisms of me are justified."[30] What Russell is arguing is that Godel's critical comments were probably true, and that we could know that because Godel had been right so often in the past about such matters. Russell's comment is not to be confused with a so-called argument from authority, by which, for example, a man will try to justify his assertions about moral matters by quoting the opinions of someone who is renowned, but who has no special competence in the field of morality. Instead, Russell's argument is a straightforward inductive argument: because something has been true in the past, it is likely to be true now. Consider one more such argument. The physicist Leon Lederman writes as follows: "By analogy, certain chemical experiments with helium and argon show no difference between them, and one could have asked why these two atoms were the same except for their different weights. The answer is that these experiments did not penetrate the outer electron shells, which of course *are* the same. Another analogy, which T. D.

---

[30] Paul Schilpp, ed., *The Philosophy of Bertrand Russell* (New York: Tudor Publishing Company, 1944), p. 74.

Lee favors and which is therefore probably right, compares mu-ness and e-ness to, say, electric and magnetic fields."[31] Professor Lederman is claiming here that a certain assertion is probably true merely because it has been made by T. D. Lee, the Nobel Prize winning physicist who, with Professor Chen Ning Yang, succeeded recently in overthrowing the parity principle of modern physics. Again, as in Russell's argument, inductive evidence suggests that a statement is true if it has been made by someone who is usually right about such matters. Of course, it is not claimed that any statement whatsoever that might be made by Godel or Lee is probably true; the claim is only that assertions about a subject in which these men have often been right in the past—namely, mathematical logic and physics—are probably true.

Now, suppose that someone or something has been right in making assertions about any subject whatsoever. For example, imagine a computer that has been fed information about all known subject matter. The computer is constructed, moreover, so that it makes only true assertions. Further, every assertion made by the computer has been independently checked and found to be true. Even statements which we had reason to believe were false have been made by the computer and have turned out to be true. Now, select any statement whatsoever (from among those not known to be true, false, or meaningless) and let it be asserted by the computer. The mere fact that the statement had been made by the computer would provide confirming evidence for the statement. Since any statement whatsoever could be asserted by the computer, any statement whatsoever can be confirmed to some extent. Moreover, if the computer were always right, and if this kind of success were maintained for years, then the fact that a statement had been made by the computer might provide very strong evidence that the statement were true. We might even reach the point where the fact that a statement had been confirmed by the computer would provide more evidence that the statement were true than any attempt at direct confirmation; just as the fact that all physicists agreed that a certain statement of physics were true might provide stronger

[31] Leon Lederman, "The Two-Neutrino Experiment," *The Columbia University Forum,* IX (Summer 1966), p. 22. This passage was pointed out to me by Jerome Weinstock.

evidence for the statement than a layman's attempt to confirm that statement directly. That reliance on the computer, however, might provide more evidential support than using more direct methods of confirmation is not necessary for the point I wish to make. All I need argue is that *some* degree of confirmation would be provided by the computer's support of a particular statement. It is also conceivable that any statement whatsoever might be confirmed to some degree by the procedure I have outlined.[32]

I conclude, then, with the following dilemma: either "meaningless" is said to mean "not directly confirmable," or it is said to mean "not indirectly confirmable." The first alternative can be shown to be false by pointing to statements which are obviously meaningful and yet are not—even in principle—directly confirmable. On the remaining alternative, however, the criterion becomes useless, for the criterion could not be used to show that any statement at all is meaningless.

3

I have tried to highlight some of the main difficulties that verificationism has had to face. Because of these difficulties, most philosophers—although not all—agree not only that we *now* have no adequate formulation of the verifiability criterion but also that we are unlikely to have one in the future. This pessimism about the future of verification is usually based on an extrapolation from past failures. All previous attempts to state an adequate criterion have failed; therefore, future attempts will probably fail. I think this pessimism is warranted, but I also believe that it can be given a more solid foundation. Thus, I have tried to provide three additional reasons why the verificationist program is likely to be a continuing failure:

1. Even if the criterion can be stated so as to be neither too liberal nor too restrictive, it will be difficult to *apply* the criterion. To prove that a statement is unverifiable is, very often, just as difficult as proving that the statement is meaningless. Unless we are provided with some way of proving

---

[32] As stated, the preceding argument might raise questions, which could prove troublesome, concerning the sense in which a computer could *understand a statement.* This has been pointed out to me by Peter Achinstein. However, such questions can be avoided by substituting an all-knowing man for a computer.

"unverifiability," therefore, the problem of proving "meaninglessness" will not be solved by stating an adequate verifiability criterion. Instead, it will merely be replaced by another problem—that of proving "unverifiability."

2. Second, and more crucial, stating an adequate criterion will be useless—unless we can show that the fact that a statement is unverifiable makes it necessary, or at least probable, that the statement is meaningless. The one feasible way of doing this would be to show that "meaningless" means, at least in part, "unverifiable." No one has ever shown this, however, and there is no reason to think that it could be shown.

3. Finally, there is positive reason for thinking that it could not be shown that "meaningless" means "unverifiable"—if "unverifiable" is understood as meaning "not *directly* confirmable." For there exist statements which are clearly meaningful and yet which are not, even in principle, directly confirmable. If "unverifiable" is understood, instead, as "not *indirectly* confirmable," then the class of statements to which the criterion would be applicable is empty. There are no statements at all, among those subject to the criterion, which are "not indirectly confirmable." Hence, even if we could adequately state the criterion, and even if we could validate its use, it would still be completely useless, for it would apply to nothing at all.

chapter iii

the category mistake argument

So far, I have argued that two widely used criteria of meaninglessness, the operationalist and verificationist criteria, are unreliable: neither can be used to prove that a statement is meaningless. I shall now discuss a third kind of criterion—a "type" or "category" criterion,[1] employed in what I shall call the "category mistake argument."

1

The category mistake argument is used primarily to expose as "meaningless" what are commonly called "category mistakes" (or, alternatively, "type mistakes"). The argument is also used to demonstrate that a certain term is ambiguous (or is being *used* ambiguously). This latter use of the concept is not new. Aristotle, for example, seems to have used it in this way (although his intentions are not quite clear), when he argued in his *Metaphysics* that the term "existence" has a different sense corresponding to each of the ten categories, and when he argued in his *Ethics* that "good" has different senses *because* it is predicated of things of different categories. Further, Whitehead and Russell used the notion of "type" in this way in *Principia Mathematica:* whenever a term seemed to be significantly predi-

---

[1] The terms "type" and "category" will be used interchangeably. Moreover, I shall speak of statements rather than sentences as being meaningless. In chapter IV I shall defend the claim, which many philosophers would find controversial, that statements can be meaningless.

cable of subjects belonging to more than one type, Whitehead and Russell took that as proof that the term was ambiguous.

The category mistake argument, then, is used in either of two ways. It is used to demonstrate that a statement is meaningless and to prove that a term is ambiguous.

In using the argument to demonstrate that a statement is meaningless, a philosopher usually (although not always) begins by stating that two terms, say X and Y, belong to different logical types. He then concludes that a third term, Z, cannot (significantly) be predicated of both terms, although it may be predicable of one. A critic of the ontological argument, for example, might argue that the terms "proposition" and "being" belong to different types; hence, the term "necessary" cannot be predicated of both of them. Since it is obviously correct to speak of necessary propositions, it must be meaningless to speak of a necessary being.

Gilbert Ryle, who has probably done more than anyone else to popularize the category mistake argument, uses the argument to show that minds cannot "exist" in the same sense that bodies "exist." To say that both minds and bodies exist, according to Ryle, is to utter nonsense.[2] More recently, Thomas Szasz, who has been influenced by Ryle, has used the argument in a similar fashion to show that mental illness is a "myth." Szasz is a psychiatrist who has been influential in the movement to replace what is sometimes known as the "disease" or "medical" model of mental illness with a "psychological" model. Dr. Szasz writes as follows:

I submit that mental illness is a myth. Bodies are physical objects; minds whatever they may be, are not physical objects. Accordingly, mental diseases (such as depression or schizophrenia) cannot exist in the sense in which bodily diseases (such as broken bones or ulcerated skins) exist.

My disbelief in mental illness does not mean that I reject any facts of human behavior. 'A myth,' says the British philosopher Gilbert Ryle, 'is not a fairy story. It is the presentation of facts belonging to one category in the idiom belonging to another. To explode a myth is accordingly not to deny facts, but to reallocate them.' To say that mental illness is a myth is

[2] For the details of Ryle's argument, see his *Concept of Mind* (New York: Barnes & Noble, 1949), p. 16.

therefore not to deny facts (such as sadness or fear) but to reallocate them (from the category of mental illness to the category of personal conduct).[3]

Szasz does not explicitly use the terms "meaningless" or "absurd," but his use of the term "cannot" and his reference to Ryle indicate that he is arguing that the term "mind" does not belong to the same type as "body." Diseases of the *body* (such as ulcerated skins) obviously do exist; therefore, diseases of the *mind* (such as schizophrenia) *cannot* exist. That is, it is absurd or meaningless to say, using "exist" in the sense in which bodily diseases exist, that mental illness exists. Mental illness, therefore, is a "myth."

As I noted earlier, the category mistake argument is used to prove ambiguity as well as nonsense. In this second use, the first step of the argument is usually the same: two terms, X and Y, are said to belong to different types. From this, it is concluded that a third term, Z, must be ambiguous, since it is predicable of both X and Y. Thus, someone might argue that "odd" must be ambiguous, since it can be predicated (significantly) of such hetero-typical terms as "number" and "person." This would, however, be a relatively uninteresting application of the argument. Of more interest and importance is the use of the argument to demonstrate, for instance, that "exist" is ambiguous.[4]

P. F. Strawson, in an interesting employment of the argument, suggests that what he calls "M Predicates" (material object predicates, such as "weighs 10 stone" and "is in the drawing room") are ambiguous because they apply to two different types of things: material objects and persons. He writes:

Indeed, if we want to locate type-ambiguity somewhere, we would do better to locate it in certain predicates like 'is in the drawing room,' 'was hit

[3] Thomas Szasz, "Mental Illness is a Myth," *The New York Times Magazine* (June 12, 1966), p. 30. Szasz repeats this argument in "Psychiatry, the Law, and Social Control," *University Review*, II (Summer 1969), p. 11. It should be pointed out, however, that Szasz supports his case by means of a number of other arguments as well. See his book *The Myth of Mental Illness* (New York: Harper & Row, 1961).

[4] See Gilbert Ryle, "Philosophical Arguments," in *Logical Positivism*, ed. A. J. Ayer (Glencoe, Ill.: The Free Press, 1959), p. 339.

by a stone,' etc. and say they mean one thing when applied to material objects and another when applied to persons.[5]

2

I shall now consider the soundness of the category mistake argument. In using it, a philosopher moves from the assumption that two terms, X and Y, are of different types to one of two conclusions: that predicating some third term, Z, of both X and Y is nonsense or that Z is ambiguous. What justifies this movement? Does it follow, for example, that "Some numbers are odd" is nonsense, or that "odd" is being used in a sense different from its sense in "Some persons are odd," merely because "number" and "person" belong to different types? Clearly it does not follow without the aid of at least one additional assumption: that terms of different types cannot share predicates (in the same sense). If it were possible for hetero-typical terms to share predicates (in the same sense), then it might be possible for "odd" to be predicable, both significantly and univocally, of "person" and "number," even if these latter two terms were distinct in type. Without at least the implicit use of this additional assumption, therefore, neither the conclusion concerning *ambiguity,* nor the conclusion concerning *nonsense,* will follow. Ryle, in fact, makes this assumption *explicit* in a passage in which he tries to show that "thinking" and "doing" are of the same type. He writes:

It also helps to upset the assumed type-difference between thinking and doing, since *only subjects belonging to the same type can share predicates.* But thinking and doing do share lots of predicates, such as 'clever,' 'stupid,' 'careful,' 'strenuous,' 'attentive,' etc.[6] (Italics added)

Suppose, then, that we follow Ryle here and assume that different types cannot share predicates. Can we now reach either of the conclu-

[5] P. F. Strawson, *Individuals: An Essay in Descriptive Metaphysics* (Garden City, N.Y.: Anchor Books, 1963), p. 101. Strawson, it should be noted, may not wish to argue that M-predicates are ambiguous. He does preface his comment with the phrase ". . . if we want to locate type-ambiguity somewhere." He may not, in fact, wish to locate type-ambiguity anywhere.

[6] Gilbert Ryle, "Knowing How and Knowing That," *Proceedings of the Aristotelian Society,* XLVI (1945–46), p. 2.

44

sions we want? Again, we cannot. If we suppose that X and Y are of different types, it still does not follow that if "X is Z" is significant, then "Y is Z" is nonsense—nor does it follow that Z is ambiguous. All that does follow, even given Ryle's assumption, is that *either* "Y is Z" is nonsense, *or* Z is ambiguous. Neither conclusion follows separately. Precisely because the category mistake argument is used in attempts to demonstrate both nonsense and ambiguity, it cannot be successfully used to demonstrate either alone, except in one way. It may at least be concluded, given Ryle's assumption, that predicating Z of X and Y *together* leads to nonsense. Ryle apparently recognizes this when he concludes only that "Minds and bodies exist" is nonsense; he does not insist that "Minds exist," or "Bodies exist," taken as separate statements are absurd ("exist," of course, would have to be used in a different sense in each statement).

In the context of other philosophic disputes, Ryle's maneuver would be of little help. The defender of the ontological argument, for example, might very well concede that "necessary" cannot be significantly predicated of "being" and "proposition" together, but all he need insist is that taken separately the predications are significant. And he can do that. All that can be proven using the category mistake argument is that *either* "necessary" is used in a nonpropositional sense in the sentence "God's existence is necessary," *or* the statement is absurd. Such a conclusion can easily be accepted by the theist; he need merely agree that "necessary" is being used in a nonpropositional sense when predicated of "God" (or "being").

So, too, an advocate of the "disease" model of psychopathology might agree that mental disease cannot exist in the same sense that physical diseases exist. He might reply, however, that just as minds exist in a different sense from that in which bodies exist, mental diseases exist in a different sense from that in which physical diseases exist. That is *not* to say that mental diseases do not exist at all (in any sense).

The point, then, is that in using the category mistake argument we can conclude at most that one of two defects is present: either a term is ambiguous, or a statement is absurd. To conclude further that one defect rather than the other is present, a supplementary argument must be supplied. I shall return to this objection later, but another objection needs to be made first.

So far, I have accepted Ryle's assumption that terms of different types cannot share predicates (in the same sense). But is the assumption true? If it is false, then the category mistake argument cannot be used even to demonstrate the disjunction: that either a certain term is ambiguous, or a certain statement is meaningless. If terms of different types *can* share predicates, then we can agree, for example, that "mind" and "body" belong to different types and nevertheless reject the conclusion that either "exists" is ambiguous, or "Minds exist" is nonsense. It is crucial for the soundness of the category mistake argument, then, that Ryle's assumption be true. Yet, it seems to me to be clearly *untrue*. Consider the following cases:

1. A term such as "interesting," for example, can be predicated of many different types of things. For instance, *parades, paradoxes,* and *people* can all be said to be interesting.

2. A number of different kinds of things can be said to be "dark"—such as *soaps, skies,* and *sheep*.

3. So, too, predicates of more philosophic interest can be shared by subjects of different types. Take, for example, "observation" and "description." Events and material objects (such as automobiles and automobile accidents) can both be "observed." They can also be "described."

4. Finally, to refer back to Strawson's argument, "persons" and "material objects" can also share predicates. Gilbert Ryle and a gatepost, for instance, can both be said to "weigh 10 stone"; so, too, both can be "six feet tall."

Either of two kinds of replies might be made to the above cases.

First, it might be argued that because the subjects cited are not really of different types, Ryle's assumption is not actually violated. In reply, however, I would claim that if we are to make type distinctions at all, then, on intuitive grounds, at least some of these terms (such as "paradoxes" and "parades," or "skies" and "sheep") surely *seem* to belong to different types. For the present, I shall merely assume that at least some of the subject-terms (within a single group) belong to different types. I shall justify this assumption later.

Second, it might be objected that although the above subjects do belong to different types, the predicates employed are ambiguous; hence, in the cases cited, hetero-typical subjects are not really sharing the same predicates. Sheep and skies are dark, for example—but in different senses. I doubt that this objection could be sustained in even one of the above cases. Since I only need a single counter-instance to refute Ryle's general assumption, I shall confine my discussion, at least for the moment, to the case of M-predicates.

Strawson, it should be pointed out, does not argue that we *must* say that M-predicates are ambiguous. He merely says that we should *"if* we want to locate type-ambiguity somewhere." That he should recommend this at all, however, suggests that he thinks it plausible to assume that terms of different types cannot share predicates. Apart from this assumption, there is nothing in his argument concerning persons that would imply that M-predicates are ambiguous. If his argument *did* imply that, we would have a good reason for rejecting it. So, too, if we can retain the assumption that hetero-typical terms cannot share predicates only by saying that M-predicates are ambiguous when predicated of persons and physical objects, then we shall have a good reason to renounce this assumption concerning hetero-typical predication. Consider what is involved in accepting Strawson's suggestion.

Suppose, for example, that we examine the M-predicate "is six feet tall." We might say that Gilbert Ryle (a person) is six feet tall and that a gatepost (a physical object) is six feet tall. Even if each assertion is true, it will still not be true that Gilbert Ryle and the gatepost are of the same height, for "six feet tall" will have a different sense in each case. In fact, it will now be nonsensical to say that they are of the same height, for the expression "are of the same height" is itself an M-predicate which cannot be significantly predicated (in the same sense) of both persons and material objects. It might be thought that we could *show* that Ryle and the gatepost are of the same height by showing that they are equal in height to a third item, say a measuring rod. If we accept Strawson's suggestion, however, we will have to conclude that it is absurd to say "We have shown Ryle and the measuring rod to be of the same height," for a measuring rod is itself a physical object and hence cannot share the predicate "is of the same height" with Gilbert Ryle, a person. Nor will the absurdities end here. For instance, if Gilbert Ryle weighs 10 stone and the gatepost weighs 10 stone, they will not be of the same weight. "Weighs 10 stone" will mean something different in each case. And, again, it will be absurd to predicate "is of the same weight" of both of them.

Such apparent absurdities could be multiplied; but there is little need to do so. The single conclusion that "weighs 10 stone" must be ambiguous when predicated of "person" and "material objects" is by itself a *reductio ad absurdum* of the belief that subjects of different types cannot share predicates.

3

Let me now re-state the two objections I have made:

1. If Ryle's assumption that terms of different types cannot share predicates in the same sense were true, this assumption, and the premise that X and Y are of different types, would still not warrant the conclusion that "if 'X is Z' is significant, then 'Y is Z' is absurd." Nor would it warrant the conclusion that "Z is ambiguous." What might be established, if Ryle's assumption were true, is that *either* absurdity *or* ambiguity is present; but to show that one rather than the other disorder is present, an additional argument would be required.

2. Ryle's assumption, apart from which the entire argument is invalid, is false. It is false to say that terms of different types cannot share predicates in the same sense.

My first objection, even if it is sound, would not in itself show that the category mistake argument is of no possible use. I shall explain why in a moment. What the objection does show is that, as the category mistake argument is *actually* used, it is unsound. Take, for example, the following case. In discussing John Dewey's philosophy of language, Max Black writes:

It seems to me that Dewey's theory of meaning is marred by two large mistakes. First, it is disconcerting to realize, as one follows his discussions, that he treats the meanings of words and the meanings of sentences as if the two belonged to the same logical category. . . . To suppose that the same formula of 'the total consequent system of social behavior' (EN191) applies equally to a statement and to a word is to overlook, in a way that is bound to lead to trouble, the radical differences in logical type between the two. Obviously, all sorts of assertions that can be made of the one generate nonsense when made of the other: it is absurd to speak of verifying or refuting a word—or, for that matter, of its social consequences.[7]

Black seems to be arguing that Dewey was speaking nonsensically— that is, he was committing a type mistake—when he spoke of words, as well as statements, as having social consequences. A statement—which is the kind of thing that can have social consequences—is not the same type of thing as a word, as is shown by the fact that some assertions about statements become nonsensical when they are made about words. If Black is arguing from the difference of types to the conclusion that Dewey's assertion is nonsense, then his argument is unsound, based on my first objection. (Although I do concede that I may be misinterpreting Black here.) Even granting that "statement" and "word" belong to different types —and conceding that this prohibits them from sharing predicates (in the same sense)—all that follows is either that "social consequences" is ambiguous, or that "Words have social consequences" is absurd. That Dewey was speaking absurdly—does not follow by itself, however, and Dewey could always reject Black's conclusion by admitting that he was using the phrase "social consequences" in two distinct senses. It is wrong, then, to use the category mistake argument (without the aid of any additional premises) to conclude that some statement is absurd or to conclude that some term is ambiguous. My first objection, I believe, demonstrates that.

What the objection does not demonstrate is that the argument is of no use at all. In some philosophical disputes, it may be quite useful to be able to conclude with the disjunction: either ambiguity or nonsense. Consider Black's discussion once more. Black seemed to be arguing that Dewey was speaking nonsensically in saying that words have social consequences; as I pointed out, the conclusion fails to follow from Black's premises. To be fair, however, Black seems to be well aware of this for he hedges his conclusion in the same paragraph. He goes on:

Hence, any account of meaning that is presented as applying to statements and their components is bound to be at least systematically

[7] Max Black, "Dewey's Philosophy of Language," *Journal of Philosophy,* LIX (1962), p. 518.

ambiguous. Recognition of the relevant differences in type would have led Dewey to see that he was using such key words as 'idea' in at least two different senses.[8]

Black seems aware, then, that Dewey could have replied that, instead of uttering nonsense, he was using "social consequences" in two senses. Black could always counter in turn, however, that at least an unclarity in Dewey's thought has been exposed, for Dewey failed to indicate his original intention. Moreover, I think that an even stronger counter-reply could be made by Black, and I assume that this stronger reply is the one that he would make. He might ask Dewey to *show* that "social consequences" has two senses, since it is not obvious that it does. I think it can be plausibly argued that—in any case where it is not self-evident that a term is ambiguous—ambiguity has to be proved and not merely assumed. Suppose I were to claim, for example, that only events, and not physical objects or persons, could be "causes"—that Hume, for example, was making a mistake when he spoke of billiard balls (physical objects) as being causes. You might reply here that my claim is false, pointing out that your brother, for example, was the cause of your mother's grief. This reply by itself, however, might not be sufficient, for while conceding that your brother was a cause of your mother's grief, I could argue that this is a different sense of "cause." The point is, however, that I would have to *argue* that "cause" is used in two senses. I could, of course, merely stipulate that I wish to use "cause" in two different senses when referring to people or physical objects and when referring to events. It would be irrelevant, however, to my original claim that only events can be causes and that Hume was guilty of a mistake in implying otherwise. I shall assume, then, that except where it is self-evident that a term is being used, or could be used, in two senses, ambiguity has to be proved and not merely assumed.

In order to answer Black, therefore, Dewey would have to show that "social consequences" does have two senses. So, too, it would not be enough for the defender of the ontological argument to say, as I said earlier, that "necessary" is used in two senses when predicated of "being"

[8] *Ibid.*, p. 519.

and "statement." He would also have to show that "necessary" does, in fact, have this second sense.

I conclude, then, that my first objection alone is not decisive in showing that the category mistake argument is of no possible use, even though it does show that as the argument is actually used (at least in some cases), it is unsound. It is unsound when the conclusion is either that ambiguity is present or that nonsense is present. My first objection is not decisive, however, because it allows that a different conclusion may be reached—namely, the disjunction: either ambiguity or nonsense. To be able to prove this disjunctive conclusion is often of considerable philosophic interest in itself.

4

If my first objection is not decisive alone, it does help to strengthen the second objection, as I shall shortly demonstrate. First, however, I should make clear that it is *not* a weakness of the second objection to assume, as I did initially, that at least some of the pairs of terms that I mentioned fall into different types. That assumption seems obviously true, unless we refuse to draw type-distinctions at all. Even if it is not, the type-differences can be *demonstrated* by appealing to Ryle's definition of "type-difference."[9] Consider the terms "automobile" and "automobile accident." We can say that "An automobile is parked in the garage." If we replace "automobile" with "automobile accident," however, we obtain the nonsensical result: "An automobile accident is parked in the garage." Since the first statement becomes nonsensical when "automobile" is replaced by "automobile accident," then, according to Ryle's definition, the two terms belong to different types. In the same way we can show that "person" and "gatepost" belong to different types. If we substitute the second for the first in "This person suffers from feelings of remorse," the

---

[9] Ryle defines "type-difference" such that two expressions are of different types if substituting one for the other turns a significant statement into a nonsensical one. See his "Categories," in *Logic and Language*, ed. Anthony Flew (Oxford: Basil Blackwell, 1961).

result is the obviously absurd statement, "This gatepost suffers from feelings of remorse."

It might be objected that the above statements are not obviously nonsensical because *no* statement is obviously nonsensical. If we say that, however, we have no way of showing that *any* two terms are of different types (unless, of course, we have some additional criterion of nonsense or meaninglessness—some criterion in addition to a type criterion—and I am assuming here that we do not). If it is argued that we have no need for a way to determine type-differences because we can simply *see* that two terms are type-distinct, I would reply as follows. If it is obvious that "mind" and "body," "Saturday" and "John," and "statement" and "word" belong to different types, it is equally obvious—no more, no less—that "person" and "gatepost" and "automobile" and "automobile accident" also belong to different types. So, too, it might be argued that although some statements are obviously nonsensical, the examples that I have cited are not. *If* "Saturday is in bed" (Ryle) and "Words are verifiable" (Black) are obviously nonsensical, then the statements I have cited—"An automobile accident is parked in the garage" and "The gatepost is suffering from feelings of remorse"—are also obviously nonsensical. Moreover, even if these statements were not obviously nonsensical, other statements could be used in their place to demonstrate the differences in type. Finally, it would not help Ryle's assumption very much even if all of the subject-terms (in each group) were of the same type. At least one of the predicate-terms I used (and there are others) can be predicated of any subject whatsoever. Anything whatsoever can be significantly said to be "interesting," although, of course, not everything *is* interesting. Hence, almost every subject-term in the language will belong to the same category and, therefore, the category mistake argument will be almost useless, or Ryle's assumption will be false. I conclude, then, that it is safe to claim that at least some of the pairs of terms I mentioned belong to different types.

The durability of my second objection, therefore, depends upon the strength of my claim that the predicates I used were univocal. Even granting that at least some of the subject-terms belong to different types, I would not have shown that Ryle's assumption is false if the predicate-terms I used were being predicated *ambiguously*. Ryle's assumption merely states that terms of different types cannot share predicates *in the same sense.* To show that automobiles and automobile accidents can be "observed" in different senses of "observe" would not be incompatible with Ryle's assumption. Nor would Ryle deny, for example, that pretty girls and logical paradoxes are "interesting," if they were "interesting" in different senses. Are the predicates I used, therefore, ambiguous? If they are, my second objection fails; if not, this objection shows that Ryle's assumption is false and, consequently, that the category mistake argument is unsound.

I have already argued that at least one of the predicates I used, namely, "weighs 10 stone," is *not* ambiguous, for to say that it is ambiguous, I argued, leads to conclusions which seem to be absurd. It seems to be absurd (not meaningless, but obviously false) to say that if Gilbert Ryle weighs 10 stone and a gatepost weighs 10 stone, then they are not of the same weight. Although this certainly *seems* to be absurd, perhaps it is not. Perhaps Ryle or Strawson, or some other philosopher who wishes to defend the use of the category mistake argument, would refuse to admit that such a conclusion is absurd because, they might argue, we have failed to realize that the predicate "weighs 10 stone" is actually used in different senses. If Ryle, or anyone else, were to reply in this manner, I would need to argue further. But here my first objection serves to support the second, for what my first objection brings out is that the category mistake argument is useful (if it is sound) only if it is useful to be able to prove the disjunctive conclusion: either absurdity or ambiguity. It is useful to be able to prove a conclusion of this kind precisely because ambiguity must be proved and not merely assumed (except, of course, where its presence is obvious). The same reasoning applies here. Thus, even if I have failed to prove that "weighs 10 stone" is *not* ambiguous, it still remains to be proved that it *is* ambiguous. Could that be proved? I have already given a reason for thinking it could not, but let us try.

5

How, in general, can we prove that a predicate is ambiguous? One way that might suggest itself is the following. Any term, C, is ambiguous if it is significantly predicable of two other terms, A and B, which are of different logical types. As I pointed out earlier, a rule of this kind has often been appealed to in past attempts to prove ambiguity. In a reply to Max Black, for example, Russell seemed to appeal to this rule.[10] Black had challenged the assumption that terms of different types cannot share univocal predicates by pointing to the predicate "is thought about." The terms "Continuity" and "Bertrand Russell" seem to belong to different types, yet we can say (significantly), "Bertrand Russell is thought about" and "Continuity is thought about." Russell replied, however, that "thinking" was being used in different senses in these two predications. His response, of course, is unsatisfactory, for in appealing to the rule that terms of different types cannot share predicates in the same sense, Russell is relying on the very assumption that Black is challenging. For the very same reason, moreover, we are prohibited from relying on this rule or assumption in trying to prove that "weighs 10 stone" is ambiguous—for this predicate, I have argued, is significantly predicable of terms of different types. Since this predicate is not obviously ambiguous, it would seem that Ryle's assumption—that terms of different types cannot share univocal predicates— is false. We may yet save Ryle's assumption by demonstrating that "weighs 10 stone," contrary to appearance, is ambiguous, but we cannot rely on his assumption to do it. We must, therefore, look for some other way to prove ambiguity.

There is another kind of rule that philosophers and laymen have relied on, at least since the time of Aristotle, in making distinctions of sense. *Roughly,* the rule is this: if B can be both affirmed and denied truly of A within the same statement, then B is ambiguous. This rule (although it needs to be stated more precisely) is nothing more than a version of, or at least an implication of, Aristotle's statement of the rule of noncontradiction. (Probably, the closest Aristotle comes to explicitly stating this as a separate rule or criterion is in Book IV, Chapter IV, of the *Metaphysics:* "And it will not be possible to be and not be the same thing, except in virtue of an ambiguity.") In applying this rule, we might say that a dark feather, for example, is both light and not light, and thus we might conclude that "light" is ambiguous. That is, "light" can mean "not heavy" or "not dark";

---

[10] See Bertrand Russell, "Reply to Criticisms," in *The Philosophy of Bertrand Russell* (Evanston, Ill.: Northwestern University Press, 1944).

hence, a dark feather is "light" (not heavy) and not "light" (not dark). This rule, however, would be of little use in our case because it applies only to predicates which are affirmed and denied of the *same* subject. We are interested in a predicate that is predicable of different subjects which belong to different types. It would not help, for example, to show that a man could both weigh 10 stone and not weigh 10 stone. We would prove at most that "weighs 10 stone" can be used in different senses when predicated of "man"; we would not show that "weighs 10 stone" is ambiguous when predicated of, say, a man and a gatepost. This rule, therefore, is of no more help than a rule of types for proving ambiguity in the case that interests us. Hence, we need to look further.

Is there a third way, then, to prove ambiguity? That is, is there another rule or criterion that we might use in attempting to prove that "weighs 10 stone" is ambiguous? One answer which has won some support among philosophers is given by Quine: there is none. Apart from a special class of cases, Quine argues, we cannot get evidence for ambiguity; and the special class of cases consists of only those in which, as with "light," the predicate can be both affirmed and denied of the same thing. Thus, in referring to the trait of "being true and false of the same thing," Quine writes: "This trait, if not a necessary condition of ambiguity of a term, is at any rate the nearest we have come to a clear condition of it."[11] I shall argue, however, that there are other criteria of ambiguity.

6

Take as an illustration a term that Quine cites. Is the term "hard" ambiguous? If we were permitted to use the type criterion, we could conclude that it is. Different types of things, namely, questions and chairs, can be said to be "hard"; but, of course, we cannot use this criterion. The "contradiction" criterion is of no help either, for it would be useful only if the *same* thing, say, a question, could be said, both significantly and truly, to be hard and not hard at the same time. That is not, however, the case. There are feathers that can be light and not light, but there are no questions

[11] W. V. O. Quine, *Word and Object* (New York: John Wiley and Sons, 1960), p. 131.

that can be both hard and not hard. Thus, if Quine is right in saying (or implying) that there is no third way of proving ambiguity, then he must say that we cannot show that "hard" is ambiguous. And that is just the position that Quine does take. He writes:

> As remarked, ambiguity may be manifested in that the term is at once true and false of the same things. This seemed to work for 'light,' but it is useless for 'hard.' For can we claim that 'hard' as applied to chairs ever is denied of hard questions, or vice versa? If not, why not say that chairs and questions, however unlike, are hard in a single inclusive sense of the word? There is an air of syllepsis about 'The chair and questions were hard,' but is it not due merely to the dissimilarity of chairs and questions? Are we not in effect calling 'hard' ambiguous, if at all, just because it is true of some very unlike things?[12]

In reply to Quine, I think that if we look at the way "hard" is actually used, we shall see that it is in fact used in different senses. Take the following three cases.

1. Suppose an examination is held in a professor's house. Now suppose that all of the chairs the students are given to sit in are hard. This implies that the chairs are not soft. Suppose the exam questions are hard as well. Should we also say, as it seems we must if "hard" means the same thing here, that because the questions are "hard," it follows that they are not soft? What would a soft question be like?

2. Suppose once more that the professor does ask hard questions. If he does, then he asks difficult questions. If the chairs are hard, does it follow that they, too, are difficult?

3. Finally, suppose that some questions are hard and some are not. Then, we can ask, for example: "Is the first question harder than the second?" "Is the fourth question, the question about the Athenian Constitution, harder than the fifth question, the question about Sparta's system of military training?" Suppose, now, that the chairs are all hard. Can we then ask: "Are all the chairs harder than the test questions?" "Is the first chair harder than the fourth question, the question concerning the Athenian Constitution?" If such questions made sense, how could they be answered?

---

[12] *Ibid.*, p. 130.

Should we say, for example, that the first chair is less *difficult* than the fourth question? Or should we say that it is *softer?*

I think the above shows that "hard" *is* used in different senses when predicated of questions and chairs. Quine, then, is wrong when he says, or at least implies, that we can show that a term is ambiguous only when the term can be both affirmed and denied of the same thing. Quine might object to each of the above three cases, but many other similar cases could be found. Moreover, many other such cases could be found for *other* terms besides "hard"; that is, other terms besides "hard" could be shown to be ambiguous by using the above procedure. Instead of citing other examples at this time, it might be more useful to see if any *general* criteria of ambiguity can be extracted from the above three cases. I think that there can. Further, I think that similar criteria can be found in the writings of Aristotle. Hence, it is to his writings that I shall now turn.

7

It is in his *Topics* that Aristotle mainly talks about ambiguity criteria. He lists there, and explains the use of, a number of criteria for detecting ambiguity—15 or 16 in all, depending on whether some very similar criteria are interpreted as being the same or different. Many of the criteria seem to be quite technical and would, I think, have little practical value. There are, however, at least three such criteria which seem to me to be useful.

Before introducing these criteria, however, a new distinction should be made and explained here. Some philosophers and lexicographers distinguish between two kinds of ambiguity: a stronger kind, in which a term has two *meanings,* and a weaker kind, in which a term has two *senses.* For example, Paul Ziff writes in his *Semantic Analysis:* "It is not the case that 'brother' in (10) has a different meaning from 'brother' in (11): it is the case that 'brother' in (10) has a different sense from 'brother' in (11)."[13] Ziff tries to explain this distinction in terms of a "tree" metaphor. To say

[13] Paul Ziff, *Semantic Analysis* (Ithaca, N.Y.: Cornell University Press, 1960), p. 179.

that a term has different senses is to say that it *branches* off: now in one direction, then in another. To say that a term has different meanings is to make a stronger claim. It is to say that the tree has not merely different branches, but also different trunks. For example, the word "division" can mean either "an army group" or "a procedure in arithmetic." Since these meanings are quite distinct, we can think of "division" as being a tree with two separate trunks. How helpful this explanation is, or even how useful the distinction is, I shall not inquire. The point I wish to make is merely this: even if a term is not obviously ambiguous in the way that "division" is —that is, even if it does not have two distinct meanings—that does not imply that the term is unambiguous. There may be present a more subtle ambiguity—the term may have two senses rather than two meanings.[14]

Aristotle also distinguishes these two kinds of ambiguity. In Book IV, Chapter II, of the *Metaphysics,* for example, he writes: "For a term belongs to different sciences not if it has different senses, but if it has not one meaning *and* its definitions cannot be referred to one central meaning." Although Aristotle makes the distinction, however, he does not always observe it. He sometimes speaks of different "meanings," when it seems clear that different "senses" would be more appropriate. In the *Topics,* in particular, he speaks of criteria for determining when a term has different *meanings;* yet, most of his examples fail to illustrate this phenomenon. The terms cited have different senses but only one meaning. Hence, in interpreting the following passages, it might be more appropriate—against the background of Aristotle's own explanations elsewhere—to read "different meanings" as "different senses."

In stating his first criterion for detecting ambiguity, Aristotle advises us "to look and see if its contrary bears a number of meanings," (*Topics* 106a). To illustrate, he uses the term "sharp." Is "sharp" being used in two senses when we speak of a sharp note and a sharp knife? To find out, we should ask if the contrary of "sharp" is different in each of the two uses. Aristotle answers that it is: the contrary of a sharp note is a *flat* note; the

---

[14] Perhaps when a term has two distinct but related senses, but not two different meanings, we should not speak of "ambiguity" at all. I am using "ambiguity," however (perhaps in a technical way), to cover both cases: the case of two different but related senses and the case of quite different meanings.

contrary of a sharp knife is a *dull* knife. He concludes, therefore, that "sharp" is ambiguous.

Aristotle's first criterion suffers from the following defect. He advises us to look for the "contrary" of a term, but he fails to tell us how "contraries" are to be identified. What, for example, is the contrary of "democracy"? Is it "oligarchy," "monarchy," "aristocracy," or something else? Or take "sharp" once more, as it is used in "sharp knives." Is "dull" its contrary or its contradictory? Either answer seems arbitrary. I think, then, that employing the troublesome notion of a "contrary" involves Aristotle in certain difficulties. I think that these difficulties are unnecessary, however, and can be avoided by deleting the notion of a "contrary." In its place, we can substitute the notion of "incompatibility relations." Instead of looking to see if a term has more than one contrary, therefore, we can merely look at the implications of using the term in different contexts to see if different things are incompatible with its different uses. For example, we don't need to ask whether "flat" is the contrary of "sharp" in "sharp notes." All we need to notice is that in saying that a *note* is sharp, we rule out the possibility of its being flat; for a *note's* being sharp is incompatible with its being flat. The same is not true of knives. A knife can be both flat and sharp; that is, it can have a blade which is flat and yet have a sharp cutting edge. When we say, therefore, that a *knife* is sharp, we imply that it is not dull, but we do not imply—as we do when we say that a *note* is sharp—that it is not flat. Thus, in one of its uses (its use with "knife") "sharpness" is incompatible with "dullness"; but in another of its uses (its use with "note"), "sharpness" is incompatible with "flatness." Hence, we can conclude that "sharp," when applied to notes and knives, is used in two senses.

A second test that Aristotle suggests is this: he tells us to look at "the classes of the predicates signified by a term" to see if they are the same. If they are not the same, Aristotle claims, the term is ambiguous (107a). What Aristotle means can be understood by looking at his examples. He points out, for instance, that "sharp" can again be seen to be ambiguous by this test. To say that a *note* is sharp is to say that it is swift, but to say that an angle is sharp is to say not that it is swift but that it is acute or less than a right angle. Roughly put, Aristotle is telling us to check whether a term in two different uses has two different synonyms (just as in using the first test, we are to see if the term has different contraries or contradictories).

As a third way of testing for ambiguity, we are told to see if a term can be compared as "more or less" or "in like manner." For two univocal uses of a term, Aristotle argues, are always comparable (107b15). For example, it seems clear that "short" is being used univocally in "This man is short" and "This tree is short." We can check this by using Aristotle's criterion: we can say, "This man is *shorter* than the tree." But when we use "short" ambiguously, as in "This man is short" and "This play is short," we cannot say, "This man is shorter than this play." If we could (correctly) say this, we could always sensibly ask, "How much shorter than the play is he?" But the question is without sense, for how could it be answered—in minutes and seconds, or in feet and inches?

8

It seems, then, that Aristotle has constructed at least three useful tests for detecting ambiguity. They are particularly useful because their employment can be justified *a priori*—which is not true of criteria in general. Where it is not true, the criteria have a limited value. Take, for example, the verifiability criterion of meaninglessness. As I pointed out in chapter II, it has proved difficult to state this criterion in such a way that it would rule out as meaningless neither too much nor too little. Even if this problem were solved, I went on to argue, another would remain. How do we justify appealing to such a criterion in any controversial case? Without such a justification, the verifiability criterion will be of limited value. In just those kinds of cases in which the criterion is designed to be used—namely, the cases in which a dispute has arisen—its employment will be prohibited. That is not true, however, of Aristotle's three ambiguity criteria. The authority of each of those criteria can be certified *before* they are appealed to in attempts to settle disputes concerning ambiguity.

The justification for using the first *two* criteria is simply this: if the implications of using a term in two different contexts are different, then we must say, in order to avoid contradiction, that the term is being used in two different senses. Take the first criterion. Suppose I wish to explain to someone what "hard" means. I might say truly, "The term 'hard' means 'not soft.' For when I say that a professor's chairs are hard, I imply that they are not soft." But I might also say truly, "The term 'hard' does *not* mean 'not soft.' When I say that a professor's examination questions are hard, I do *not* imply that they are not soft. (If it is true of any question whatsoever that it is not soft, then, of course, a hard question is not soft. That does not mean that I *imply* that a question is not soft when I say that it is hard; for even a question that was *not* hard would be not soft.)" I cannot say truly both (1) that "hard" means "not soft" and (2) that "hard" does not mean "not soft"—unless "hard" is being used in (1) and (2) in two different senses. If "hard" were not being used in different senses, we could say that "hard" both means and does not mean "not soft." That, of course, would be self-contradictory. Hence, we are forced to conclude that "hard" has two senses. Moreover, in general, and not just in the case of "hard," if the *negative* implications of using a term in two different contexts are different—i.e., if different things are *incompatible* with the different uses of the term—then the term is used in different senses.

The same kind of justification can be given for use of the second criterion. If the *positive* implications of using the term are different in different contexts—that is, if the term has different synonyms—then the term is ambiguous. Look at "hard" once more. In explaining what this term means, I might say truly, "The term 'hard' means 'difficult,' for when I say that a professor's examination questions are hard, I imply that they are difficult." I might also say truly, "The term 'hard' does not mean 'difficult.' When I say that a chair is hard, I do not imply that it is difficult." Using the same reasoning as before, then, we can conclude once again that "hard" has two senses. If it did not, then it would be true that "hard" both does and does not mean "difficult."

The third test, the comparison test, can be justified in the following way. In the first place, if a term *passes* the test, then it need not be ambiguous (at least not in the uses being considered). Of no term whatsoever is it true that it both must be ambiguous when used with two other terms and yet can be used comparatively with these two terms. It is easy to see why. Assume, for the moment, that the term "short" must be used in different senses when used with "pygmy" and "lifespan." "Short" must, therefore, have different senses in (1) "This pygmy is short" and (2) "This lifespan is short." Using subscripts, we can mark these two senses as "short$_1$" and "short$_2$." Now, suppose we try to use "short" comparatively. If we say, for example, that "This pygmy is shorter than his lifespan," we must be using either "short$_1$" or "short$_2$"—assuming that "short" has no third sense. If we are using "short$_1$," however, it is false that "short" must be ambiguous when used with "pygmy" and "lifespan," for it is used in a single sense in the statement. The same result will occur if we are using "short$_2$." Moreover, it will not matter even if there is a third sense of "short," for at least in this third sense, "short" will be employable with "pygmy" and "lifespan"—and that is sufficient to falsify the assumption that "short" *must* be ambiguous when used with these two subjects. In general, then, if a term, C, can be used comparatively with two other terms, A and B, then it is false that C must be ambiguous when used with these two terms. So far, all this shows is that a term is *not* ambiguous—or at least need not be ambiguous—but that at least provides a test for univocality. If any term, C, can be used comparatively with A and B, then the term is, or can be, univocal when used with A and B. Thus, if it does make sense to say, "This pygmy is shorter than his lifespan," then "short" is, or can be, used in a single sense in both "This pygmy is short" and "This lifespan is short." Moreover, if a term fails the test in some context, and yet can be used comparatively in other contexts, then the failure can be explained in terms of ambiguity (assuming no other explanation is available). The term "short," for example, can be used comparatively in some contexts. We *can* say, for example, that Joseph Stalin was shorter than Charles DeGaulle. Yet, it cannot be so used in certain other contexts. For example, it cannot —contrary to my earlier assumption—be used comparatively with "pygmy" and "lifespan." It makes no sense to say "This pygmy is shorter than his lifespan." If we could say that (significantly), then we could sensibly ask, "How much shorter than his lifespan is he?" But this question is obviously nonsensical. If it is not nonsensical, then how is it to be answered: in years and days, or in feet and inches? Where no other explanation is available, then, it seems reasonable to explain the failure of a term to function comparatively by saying it is ambiguous. It seems reasonable to explain, for example, why "short" cannot be used comparatively with "pygmy" and "lifespan" by saying that it is predicable of these two subjects only in different senses.

I conclude, therefore, that use of the first two tests for ambiguity can be justified *a priori*. The use of the third test as a univocality, rather than an ambiguity, test can be given a similar justification. Moreover, as an ambiguity test, this third test can be given some justification, even if the justification is weaker than it is in the other cases.

9

Contrary to what Quine claims, then, there are tests for determining ambiguity besides the one test he allows, the "contradiction" test. What we now need to see is whether these tests can be used in demonstrating the ambiguity of "weighs 10 stone."

I argued earlier that two different types of things, a person and a gatepost, could both be said to "weigh 10 stone." If "weighs 10 stone" can then be predicated of each subject in the *same sense,* Ryle's assumption—that terms of different types cannot share univocal predicates—is therefore false. If Ryle's assumption is false, then the category mistake argument is unsound. What needs to be determined, therefore, is whether "weighs ten stone" is being used in the same sense in such statements as "This person weighs 10 stone" and "This gatepost weighs 10 stone."

Using the first test, to say that a person weighs 10 stone is to imply that the person does not weigh seven stone, and it is also to imply that the person does not weigh 13 stone. This, however, will not help. The negative implications of predicating "weighs 10 stone" of a gatepost are exactly the same. Thus, to say that a gatepost weighs 10 stone is to imply that the gatepost does not weigh seven stone and also that it does not weigh 13 stone. Moreover, I think this will be found to be true of *all* of the negative implications of using "weighs ten stone": those which hold when "weighs 10 stone" is predicated of a person will also hold when "weighs 10 stone" is predicated of a gatepost. The first test, then, will not show that "weighs 10 stone" is ambiguous.

Moreover, I think that the same is true of the second test. To say that a person weighs ten stone is to imply that the person weighs 140 pounds, for in the British system of weights and measures, "1 stone" is equivalent to "14 pounds;" hence, "10 stone" is equivalent to "140 pounds." To say that a gatepost weighs 10 stone is also to imply that it weighs 140 pounds. Once more, I think the same will be found to be true of *all* of the positive implications of using "weighs 10 stone": those which hold when "person" is the subject will also hold when "gatepost" is the subject. The second test, therefore, will also fail to show that "weighs 10 stone" is ambiguous. One test remains, the comparison test.

Can "weighs 10 stone" be used comparatively? I think that it obviously can. We can say that if King Farouk weighs 20 stone and John Foster Dulles weighs 10 stone, then *King Farouk weighs 10 stone more than John Foster Dulles*. The expression "weighs 10 stone," therefore, is the kind of expression to which our third test can be applied. To apply the test, then, we need to determine whether "weighs 10 stone" can be used comparatively with "person" and "gatepost." If it is obvious that it cannot, or if we can *show* that it cannot, then we will have reason for concluding that "weighs 10 stone" is ambiguous. Neither alternative, however, seems plausible. It is not obviously nonsensical to say that "This person weighs 10 stone more than this gatepost." We might, in fact, make such a statement if we wished to compare the weight of King Farouk to the weight of a 10-stone gatepost. If the comparison is not obviously nonsensical, I do not think it could be shown to be so either. We could bring out the absurdity of our earlier comparison—that a pygmy is shorter than his lifespan—by asking, "How much shorter is he?" Such a procedure in this case fails to exhibit any such obvious absurdity. We *can* sensibly ask: "How much more than the gatepost does King Farouk weigh?" Someone might, in fact, ask this question if he were unfamiliar with the use of the expression "weighs 10 stone." Moreover, the correct answer to the question does not seem at all problematic. It is not *obviously* nonsensical—although I am not saying that such a reply is significant—to say that King Farouk weighs 140 pounds more than the gatepost. Since it is not obviously nonsensical, then it cannot be used to show that "This person weighs 10 stone more than this gatepost" is meaningless. If this latter statement is not obviously nonsensical, and if it cannot be shown to be nonsensical, then the third test will also fail to show that "weighs 10 stone" is ambiguous. We still have no reason, therefore, for holding that this expression is used in different senses when predicated of "person" and "gatepost." Moreover, I think we now have positive reason for saying that the expression *is* being used here in a single sense and that the statement "This person weighs 10 stone more than this gatepost" is significant. Suppose, for example, that we were to use a balance to weigh King Farouk. We might place a 10-stone gatepost plus a 10-stone weight on one end of the balance and place King Farouk on the other end. If the scale were to balance, we would know that the 10-stone weight plus the gatepost were equal in weight to the weight of King Farouk. We might then conclude (referring to King Farouk): "This person weighs 10 stone more than the gatepost." If we can significantly say this, then we can apply our third test to show that "weighs 10 stone" *must* be univocal (in this context). Our third test tells us that if an expression can be used comparatively with two terms then it must be possible to use this expression with these two terms in a single sense. We may conclude, then, that "weighs ten stone" is not (or at least, need not be) ambiguous when predicated of "person" and "gatepost." I have already argued that "person" and "gatepost" belong to different types, if we accept Ryle's definition of "type difference." Hence, Ryle's assumption—that terms of different type cannot share univocal predicates—is false; and since this assumption is false, then the category mistake argument, which employs this assumption as one of its central premises, is unsound. We cannot show that a statement is meaningless, therefore, by use of this argument.

10

The fatal weakness of the category mistake argument is its essential reliance on the central assumption that terms of different types cannot share predicates in the same sense. The assumption is crucial, as I have already argued, because without it even the disjunctive conclusion "ambiguity or absurdity" could not follow from the premise that two terms are of different types and a third term is being predicated of both of them. Reject this assumption, then, and the whole argument collapses. Once we are allowed to reject this assumption, we can allow, for example, that "mind" and "body" are of different types, and yet still not be forced to the conclusion either that "exist" is ambiguous, or that "Mind exists" or "Bodies exist" is nonsense. If this central assumption is crucial, it is also false, and, hence, deserves to be rejected. I have tried to show that this is so by presenting one convincing case of two hetero-typical terms sharing a univocal predicate: the case of "person" and "gatepost" sharing "weighs 10 stone." I think there are many similar cases, as I indicated earlier, including "interesting" (which can be predicated of almost every possible subject) and "observed" (which can be predicated of both events and physical objects). It appears, then, that the category mistake argument needs the above assumption *and* that the assumption is false.

Even the most unhealthy arguments can be saved if we are willing to offer the required remedies. One remedy in this case might be to substitute a weaker assumption for the above false assumption and to restrict the scope of the argument. I should now like to consider briefly one interesting attempt to apply such a remedy.

11

Fred Sommers, in an interesting series of articles, has tried to show that the "strong" assumption of Russell and Ryle is false and that a weaker version can serve as its replacement. The strong assumption, once more, is that there is no predicate, P, which can be predicated in the same sense of two subjects of different types. Moreover, given Ryle's definition of "type-difference," if some other predicate, Q, can be applied (significantly) to one subject and not the other, then these two subjects are of different types. If we combine the strong assumption with Ryle's definition of "type-difference," then we get the following rule, Rule R:

(R) If P and Q are univocal predicates, then there are no two things, a and b, such that P applies to both while Q applies to one and not the other.

What this rules out, for example, is "exist" applying univocally to "mind" and "body" while, say, "is heavy" applies to "body" but not to "mind."

What Sommers does is to replace Rule R with a weaker rule, Rule T, which reads:

(T) If P and Q are univocal predicates, then there can be no three things, a, b and c such that P applies to a and to b but not to c while Q applies to b and to c but not to a.[15]

Rule T retains the same notion of type-difference: a and b are of different types if any predicate, c, makes sense with a but not with b. It rejects, however, the "strong" assumption "that hetero-typical terms can *never* share univocal predicates" and substitutes a weaker version under which there are some univocal predicates that can be shared by hetero-typical subjects. The term "interesting" is such a predicate. What T does, in effect, is to allow one to rule in advance which predicates can cover subjects of different types and which cannot. The term "interesting," for example, can be applied to subjects of different types simply because we cannot find three things, a, b, and c, such that "interesting" makes sense with a and b, but not with c. We cannot because there is no such c: anything at all can be significantly said to be "interesting." In cases such as this—in which a predicate can be significantly applied to any subject whatsoever—the rule cannot be invoked; moreover, the rule tells us that in advance. This restricts the scope of the rule, and, hence, restricts the scope of any argument which makes use of the rule. This restriction also makes the rule much more difficult to refute.

The following example illustrates how the rule might be applied. Suppose we have three subjects: buildings, men, and arguments. Now we need to find two predicates, such that one applies to the first two subjects but not to the third, and the other applies only to the second two subjects. For example, "tall" applies to buildings and men, but not to arguments; and "rational" applies to men and arguments, but not to buildings. In that case, all of the conditions for applying the rule are fulfilled. We are forced to conclude, then, (in order to avoid violating the rule) that one of the terms involved, either a subject-term ("men," "arguments," or "build-

[15] Fred Sommers, "Predicability," in *Philosophy in America,* ed. Max Black (Ithaca, N.Y.: Cornell University Press, 1965), pp. 265, 266.

ings") or a predicate-term ("tall" or "rational"), is ambiguous.[16] For example, we might "split"—that is, describe as ambiguous—the subject-term "man." We might say that when we speak of "rational men" and "tall men," we are using "men" in different senses. In this particular case, however, it would seem more reasonable to split "rational" instead of "men" and conclude that "rational" has two senses in "rational argument" and "rational man." This is, in fact, the choice Sommers makes when he discusses this case.[17]

12

I think it must be conceded that Rule T is much more reliable than Rule R, which breaks down in many cases. It is difficult to find cases in which Rule T does fail to work properly. Nevertheless, although Sommers' rule is certainly superior in some ways to Rule R, I think it, too, is defective. For lack of space, I shall not attempt to discuss in detail what I consider to be both its merits and its weaknesses; instead, I shall simply list three objections.

1. In using Sommers' rule (Rule T), we have to employ five terms: three subject-terms and two predicate-terms. Under certain initial conditions, the rule tells us that one of these terms is ambiguous, but it fails to tell us *which* is the guilty term. For example, assume that at least one of the following is ambiguous: "rational," "tall," "building," "man," or "argument." How do we decide which one? Sommers chooses the first term, "rational"; moreover, his choice may be *obviously* correct. In other cases, however, where a live dispute about ambiguity exists, the choice may not be obvious at all. It is precisely because the answer is not obvious that a rule is most often needed, and in such cases, appeal to the rule will not settle the dispute. Nor are these the only such cases. For the rule is also

---

[16] This assumes that the initial conditions are as I described them; however, we could re-describe these conditions if none of the ambiguity options seemed attractive. By "re-describing the initial conditions," I mean declaring that one of the predications is not significant but is meaningless. For example, I said that "rational" applies to arguments; rather than say this, we might decide that it is meaningless to speak of "rational arguments."

[17] See Fred Sommers, "A Program for Coherence," *Philosophical Review,* LXXIII (1964), p. 525.

used, just as the category mistake argument is employed, to enforce claims about meaninglessness as well as ambiguity. New options and new escape routes are thereby created for any disputant. For example, in the above case, the rule can be invoked to prove ambiguity only if the following initial conditions are met: we must agree that it is significant to speak of a rational man and of a rational argument, but nonsense to speak of a rational building; and we must also agree that it is significant to speak of a tall building and a tall man, but nonsense to speak of a tall argument. But a disputant may not agree that *all* of these conditions hold: he may say, instead, that one of the assumed significant predications is not significant, or that one of the supposed absurd predications is not absurd. Such an option may not be a live option in a case where there is no disagreement in the first place; but that will not be so in cases in which a dispute has arisen. Take the case of "exist." Ryle claims that this term is ambiguous and Quine claims that it is not. Moreover, Sommers agrees with Quine because he claims that Rule T cannot be invoked to show that "exist" is ambiguous.[18] The reason, Sommers thinks, is that "exist" is like "interesting": we cannot find three things, a, b, and c, such that "exists" makes sense with a and b, but not with c, because any subject whatsoever can be said to "exist."

The question at issue, however, is whether anything whatsoever can be said to "exist" in a single sense of "exist." Why could not Ryle argue in the same manner Sommers does with "rational?" There are three subjects —buildings, men, and arguments—and two predicates—"exist" and "rational." "Rational" makes sense with "men" and "arguments," but not with "buildings"; and "exists" makes sense with "men" and "buildings," but not with "arguments" (it makes no sense to speak of arguments existing in the same sense in which men and buildings exist). We can now invoke the rule, and split not "rational" but "exist." We can say, therefore, that "exist" is ambiguous in "men exist" and "arguments exist." Quine, of course, would not be convinced by the argument, for he would simply deny that it makes no sense to speak of both arguments and buildings "existing" in the same sense.

Rule T, in short, is much too weak to resolve disputes in which there

[18] See Fred Sommers, "Types and Ontology," *Philosophical Review,* LXXII (1963), p. 359.

would be disagreement either about the initial conditions or about which of the five terms is ambiguous. Sommers, in fact, claims only that his rule is a "coherence rule"—if you accept such and such conditions, then you must accept such and such a result. The rule does not by itself determine that a given statement is meaningless or that a particular term is ambiguous. Nevertheless, Sommers claims that use of his rule does provide both a "powerful technique for doing 'logical geography' " and "a satisfactory clarification procedure for enforcing ambiguity at the type level." Given the many escape routes that his rule allows, however, I think that both claims are open to doubt.

2. Rule T, then, is too weak to be relied on in many disputes about either ambiguity or meaninglessness. I am not asserting, however, that there are no disputes at all in which Rule T would be useful, assuming that the rule is valid. What I now want to show is that even in cases where the rule might be applied, its use entails certain difficulties.

Sommers claims that his rule can be applied in certain disputes about the mind-body problem. In fact, he claims that if we grant that there are minds or egos, then use of his rule forces us to accept Cartesian dualism.[19] This conclusion in itself should tell against our using the rule *if*—as I think is the case—there are independent good reasons for not accepting Cartesian dualism. Even apart from this, there are other difficulties, for Sommers thinks we can argue for Cartesian dualism in the following manner. Rule T, once more, tells us that "there are no three subjects, a, b, and c, such that of two univocal predicators, P and Q, P applies to a and b but not to c, and Q applies to b and c but not to a." We now have to find three subjects and two predicates which can meet these conditions. Sommers suggests the subjects: an ego (or alternatively, a pure spirit, such as God), Smith, and a stone. Now the P-predicate, "is thinking about Vienna," applies to the ego and to Smith, but not to a stone. Further, an M-predicate, such as "is heavy" applies to Smith and a stone, but not to an ego. Under these conditions, Rule T can be applied, and will instruct us that one of the five terms is ambiguous. The question then becomes: *which* of the five is ambiguous? P. F. Strawson, whose views I referred to earlier, thinks that

---

[19] See Sommers, "Program for Coherence," p. 524.

the Cartesian error is to designate the wrong term, or kind of term, as ambiguous. Thus, he writes: "That is, if we are to avoid the general form of this error, we must not think of 'I' or 'Smith' as suffering from type ambiguity."[20] Strawson suggests, instead, that we pick a term such as "is heavy" (or "weighs 10 stone"), and say that it has different senses when applied to a person and a material object. I have already argued against accepting Strawson's suggestion. Sommers also thinks that Strawson's suggestion is wholly unacceptable and thus concludes that the "Cartesian error" is not an error at all: we *should* say that "Smith" is ambiguous. Further, the fact that we should split "Smith" rather than "is heavy" shows, Sommers contends, that Descartes' doctrine is true and that Strawson's doctrine is incoherent.[21]

Saying what Sommers says, however, generates new difficulties—apart from those that trail along with Cartesianism. For example, Sommers' rule is designed to help us make ambiguity judgments, but in what sense can "Smith," or any other proper name, be "ambiguous"? If we agree that proper names have no meaning (or connotation) in the sense that words do, then how could "Smith" have even one meaning, let alone two? Of course, we may want to claim in the first place that proper names do have meaning in the same sense that words do; however, there are some seemingly obvious difficulties which would have to be faced if we were to say that proper names have meaning. For example, a word such as "stone" has a correct use, but does "Smith" have a correct use? It would be a mistake to refer to D. H. Lawrence as "Smith," since that was not Lawrence's name, but would it be a linguistic mistake? Would a mistake of this kind even tend to show that I did not know how to use a term in the English language? Moreover, if I learn enough English, I learn how to use the word "stone," but in learning English do I, or need I, also learn how to use the name "Smith"? If so, what *is* its correct use? Maybe these difficulties are only apparent difficulties and would succumb to a proper analysis. Still, any rule that forces us to say that proper names are ambiguous should be viewed with suspicion until those difficulties can be eliminated.

There is a further difficulty. Suppose we substitute "I" for "Smith" in

[20] Strawson, *Individuals*, p. 101.
[21] See Sommers, "Predicability," p. 266.

the above case. The result will be the same. Use of Rule T will lead us to the conclusion that the term "I" is ambiguous (assuming, as Sommers does, that the other alternatives are even more unacceptable). Now what does this mean? The term "I" might, perhaps, be described as "referentially ambiguous," which is a gaudy way of saying that the term "I" can be used to refer to many speakers. That is also true of the term "speaker" and does not mean that "speaker" is ambiguous. Apart from pointing out that "I" can have more than one referent, I am not sure what would be meant by saying that "I" is ambiguous. If what is being said is that "I" has different senses, in the same way that "light" does, then I think we should simply reject the claim. If we do, then we must also reject the rule that would force this conclusion upon us.

3. Even if we can make sense of saying that "Smith" and "I" are ambiguous, however, I think there is a further, decisive reason for rejecting Rule T: what the rule tells us is simply not true. It is not true that "there are no three subjects, a, b, and c, such that of two univocal predicates, P and Q, P applies to a and b but not to c, and Q applies to b and c but not to a." In just the case in which Sommers tries to apply the rule, the mind-body case, there *are* three such subjects: the ego, Smith, and a stone. Sommers claims that one of these subjects, "Smith," does not qualify because "Smith" is ambiguous. It can be shown, however, that this is not so. If it were, we would have to say that a statement such as "That fat boy, Mr. Smith, is a boy who thinks a lot" is meaningless, when it is obviously not meaningless. "Smith" is therefore not ambiguous.

Professor Sommers anticipates the above kind of argument, and his remarks are worth quoting:

> Of course this argument against Descartes is an ordinary language argument. Descartes is recommending that we reconstrue all statements about fat thoughtful people. He would say that such statements—if they are taken to be about individuals—have as little meaning as the one about the young lady who came home in a sedan chair and a flood of tears.[22]

I am puzzled about why Sommers thinks the above kind of argument deserves to be called "an ordinary language argument," while he apparently

[22] *Ibid.*, p. 270.

72

does not think that is true of his own arguments against Pyle's "strong" type assumption. But this is relatively unimportant. What is important is that statements about fat, thoughtful people are not meaningless; and since they are not, Sommers' rule—which implies that they are—is defective. Sommers' rule incorporates an assumption about the inability of hetero-typical terms to share certain univocal predicates. Although this assumption is weaker than the "strong" assumption that "hetero-typical subjects can *never* share univocal predicates," it is false.

We may, of course, wish to accept Descartes' recommendation that we reconstrue statements about fat, thoughtful people. We might do this, for instance, if Descartes could provide some independent and convincing argument to show that such statements, contrary to appearances, really are meaningless. Until some such argument is provided, it is not the statements that will be rejected, but rather the rule whose use entails that such apparently meaningful statements are really meaningless. Moreover, it is not just statements about fat, thoughtful people which will have to be "reconstrued" if we accept Descartes' recommendation. Statements such as "Losing a great deal of *weight* affected his ability to *think*" and "I *wish* it were easy for me to gain *weight*" will also have to be "reconstrued" as meaningless. Accepting such a recommendation, then, will not be easy.

There are, moreover, other cases to which Rule T does not apply. For example, consider the three subjects: a headache, a parade, and a pretty girl. The predicate "started at 3 P.M." applies to the first two but not to the third; and the predicate "was watched" applies to the second two but not to the first. All of the conditions of Rule T are fulfilled, and yet none of the five terms is ambiguous. Once again the rule breaks down. Given what Sommers says elsewhere about perceptual terms, I suppose he might reply here that "watch" should be considered ambiguous.[23] He might say that we do not watch parades in the same sense in which we watch pretty girls. This kind of reply, however, fails to work in this case, even if it does work in the case of other perceptual terms. For in this case, we can show that "watch" is univocal by using the comparison criterion discussed earlier. Assume, for example, that we are watching an American Legion parade consisting only

[23] *Ibid.*

of male marchers. Suppose, however, that although there are no pretty girls in the parade, there are a number of them standing on the sidelines. In that case, we might "spend more time watching the pretty girls than the parade." If we can do this, then "watching" can be used univocally with both "parade" and "pretty girl."

The same is true of "began at 3 P.M." My head may begin to hurt at the very same time that the parade begins—for example, at 3 P.M. In that case, I might say "My headache and the parade both began at 3 P.M." So, too, I might say that "My headache and the parade both lasted for an hour." This shows that the second predicate, "began at 3 P.M.," is also univocal, just as "watch" is univocal.

13

I have not tried to show that Sommers' technique for detecting type mistakes could not be developed further, just as Sommers has developed further the techniques of Russell and Ryle. If it could be developed further, then perhaps Rule T could provide a satisfactory method of settling disputes about meaninglessness and ambiguity. I do doubt, though, that this could be done. In order to improve a rule such as Rule T, it would have to be made more and more complex, just as Russell's and Ryle's original rule (or assumption) that "hetero-typical terms can never share predicates" was improved upon by replacing it with a more complicated rule. As the rule becomes more and more complex—as the number of conditions for applying the rule are increased—the cases to which the rule can be applied become fewer and fewer. I have already indicated that Sommers' rule cannot be applied in many disputes, such as the dispute about the alleged ambiguity of "exists," simply because agreement could not be reached about the conditions for applying the rule. To render the rule more complex still would be to diminish further its range of application, perhaps to the point where the rule would be useless.

Nevertheless, perhaps a rule could be developed which would be both practical and reliable. I have not tried to show a priori that this could not be done. What I have tried to show, instead, is this: (1) The category mistake argument, which is the standard argument used in proving the presence of category mistakes, is unsound. It is unsound because it employs Ryle's assumption that no hetero-typical terms can share univocal predicates, an assumption which is demonstrably false. (2) The most sophisticated attempt that I am aware of to improve upon the category mistake argument also fails for various reasons. One of these reasons is that the assumption which Sommers substitutes for Ryle's type-assumption is also false.

I think we are justified in concluding, therefore, that *at present*—regardless of what may come later—we do not have a satisfactory technique for identifying category mistakes. What, then, becomes of the concept of a category mistake? Should we abandon its use? Or does such a notion still have a useful role to play in philosophic discourse?

14

The basic insight, I think, of Russell, Ryle, and Sommers concerning category mistakes is that very often we do use a term in different senses when we predicate it of radically different kinds of things. We do, for example, use "odd" in different senses when we predicate it of numbers and persons. Moreover, I would like to suggest that quite often it is *because* the items are of a radically different kind that we say that the term predicated of them has two senses. It is *because* numbers and persons are so radically different that it is hard to see how they could both be "odd" in the same sense. If this hypothesis is correct (not necessarily in this particular case, but in some cases), then we might *explain* why either ambiguity or nonsense is present in some cases by pointing out that hetero-typical predication is involved. We cannot *argue* simply from a difference in type to a conclusion that either ambiguity or nonsense is involved, for that is not true in all cases. Terms of different types, as I argued earlier, can share univocal predicates in at least some cases. Once we know that ambiguity or nonsense is present (once we have established this on independent grounds), then we may be able to explain the presence by using the notion of a type mistake. I cannot prove, for example, that an accident has occurred merely by pointing out that careless driving is present, for careless driving does not always cause accidents. Nevertheless, I might explain why a certain accident has occurred, once I know that it has in fact occurred, by pointing out that the driver was driving carelessly.

This is one possible use, then, of the concept of a category mistake. After it has been argued on independent grounds that a term is ambiguous or that a statement is meaningless, we might be able to explain the presence of ambiguity or of nonsense by pointing out that hetero-typical predication is involved.

Moreover, I think that the notion of a category mistake has a second useful function. Even if it cannot be used to demonstrate that either ambiguity or nonsense is present, I think it can be used to provide some evidence, though not conclusive evidence, for such a conclusion. Perhaps this is what Ryle has in mind, when he writes in one of his later works:

I think it is worthwhile to take some pains with this word 'category,' but not for the usual reason, namely that there exists an exact, professional way of using it, in which, like a skeleton-key, it will turn all our locks for us; but rather for the unusual reason that there is an inexact, amateurish way of using it in which, like a coal-hammer, it will make a satisfactory knocking noise on doors we want opened to us. It gives the answer to none of our questions but it can be made to arouse people to the questions in a properly brusque way.[24]

We can, for example, at least create a suspicion that "necessary" has two senses in "necessary being" and "necessary statement" by pointing out that a being and a statement are very different kinds of things. Once the suspicion has been created, further argument will be needed; but at least in trying to establish the initial doubt, use of the notion of a type or category mistake can be helpful. I conclude, therefore, that the concept of a category mistake does have a useful role to play in philosophic discourse, even though it cannot be used in any simple or decisive way to settle disputes about meaninglessness or ambiguity.

Where does this leave us in our search for adequate criteria for

[24] Gilbert Ryle, *Dilemmas* (Cambridge: Cambridge University Press, 1954), p. 9. The quotation suggests that Ryle no longer accepts the assumption that only subjects belonging to the same type can share univocal predicates. Thus, even if he did employ the category mistake argument in *The Concept of Mind* (and even here I may be misinterpreting him), he would probably not accept such an argument today.

"meaninglessness"? I have examined the three kinds of criteria that have most often been appealed to in claims about meaninglessness: the operationalist, the verificationist, and, finally, the category or type criterion. Each of these has proved defective. It seems, then, that we still do not have an adequate technique for locating and identifying nonsense. Should we abandon our use of this concept? Should we cease speaking of "meaningless statements?"

I shall attempt to answer these questions in the final chapter, where I shall also attempt to answer other general questions about the concept of meaninglessness. In anticipation, however, I might point out that, although none of the usual criteria of meaninglessness have proved adequate, it is not true that we have been unable to find any criteria at all. The three criteria of ambiguity which I tried to develop when discussing the term "hard" can also serve as criteria of meaninglessness because of the relation between meaninglessness and ambiguity. I shall have more to say about this relation, and about the use of these criteria, in the last chapter.

chapter iv

meaningless statements

In this chapter, I shall defend an assertion I made in the previous chapter: that statements, not sentences, are the kinds of things that can be meaningless.

1

Statements should be said to be meaningless (or not meaningless) for very much the same reasons that statements, and not sentences, should be said to be either true or false. To put it (for the moment) quite obscurely: "meaningless" and "true or false" are on the same semantic level. Both apply, or fail to apply, to the same kinds of things. Even if "true," "false," and "meaningless" do apply to the same kinds of things, however, that in itself does not show that statements, but not sentences, should be said to be meaningless. It is not at all obvious—some philosophers, in fact, explicitly deny—that statements, and not sentences, should be said to be "true" or "false" either. Many philosophers do think it correct to speak of true or false sentences.[1] It will not do, therefore, to argue simply that the reasons for describing statements rather than sentences as true or false also warrant our describing statements rather than sentences as meaningless. What has

[1] For example, Theodore Drange writes: "Some philosophers would object to this, saying that sentences are not the type of thing that could be true or false, that only propositions (i.e., what sentences express) can be said to be true or false. But I have never seen any good argument for this view." See his *Type Crossings* (The Hague: Mouton & Co., 1966), p. 6.

to be shown, in the first place, is that such reasons are good reasons. Hence, before building on the assertion that statements, but not sentences, can be true or false, I shall attempt to show that these reasons are good reasons.

I should first point out two things that I am *not* denying.

I am not denying that the term "sentence" can be used in the same way, or in very much the same way, as I shall be using the term "statement." If "sentence" is used to mark the same distinctions, or very much the same distinctions, as I shall mark by use of the term "statement," then it matters little whether we say that statements, or sentences, are true (or false): either terminology would be appropriate. The distinctions to be observed, not the terminology used in observing them, are important. The primary distinction I have in mind, to put it quite roughly, is between *what is said* when someone states or asserts something, (what is said being the statement) and *the string of words* used in making the statement (the string of words being the sentence). It is the string of words, then, that I assume someone is referring to when he asserts that sentences can be true or false. That is what I shall mean when I speak of the "ordinary use" of the term "sentence" (even though, in fact, this may not be the ordinary use of "sentence" at all).

I also do not wish to deny that for certain purposes one need not draw the distinctions I shall be drawing. Where there is no need to draw such distinctions, it may be quite correct to speak of sentences, or even of sentences *and* statements, as being either true or false. A logician, for example, may use "sentence" in very different ways from that in which I am using "statement," and yet may correctly speak of sentences as being true or false. Again, I am not denying that possibility.

To show that in the ordinary use of "sentence," sentences (in contrast to statements, assertions, and the like) can be neither true nor false, it is useful to turn to an argument used by Paul Ziff.[2] His argument runs as follows. Suppose at time A, I say, "The cat is on the mat," and at time A, the cat *is* on the mat. If sentences can be true, then the sentence "The cat is on the mat" is true. Suppose, however, that I say at time B, "The cat is on

---

[2] Ziff, *Semantic Analysis,* p. 119.

the mat," and at time B, the cat is *not* on the mat. Then the sentence "The cat is on the mat" is not true. Since one and only one sentence is in question, the sentence "The cat is on the mat" will be said to be both true and not true; therefore, it is neither. By use of a similar argument it could be shown that a sentence is neither false nor not false. We can therefore conclude that sentences are neither true nor false.

Ziff's argument, however, is not conclusive. There are ways other than denying that sentences are either true or false to avoid the contradiction. For one thing, we may introduce a technical terminology and speak of sentence "types" and sentence "tokens." We may then say, in the above case, that although there is present only one sentence type, there are two sentence tokens—that is, there are two instances, or tokens, of the sentence type, "The cat is on the mat." Furthermore, it might be argued, it is sentence tokens, not sentence types, that are either true or false. Hence, the contradiction is avoided because "true" and "not true" apply, in this case, to two different sentence tokens.

I think it should be noted that once we introduce this technical distinction between sentence type and sentence token, we are already altering the "ordinary" use of "sentence." I do not think that we would ordinarily distinguish two different sentences in the above case. Of more importance is a different point, which Ziff makes: the introduction of this technical terminology, although of some help in the above case, will not be adequate in other cases. Suppose, for example, that we write the sentence "The cat is on the mat" on a blackboard, which is in a room containing a cat and a mat. Since a sentence is enduring entity, the same sentence may remain on the blackboard for a certain length of time. Moreover, only one sentence token, only one instance of the sentence type, will be present. Now suppose that during the period in which the sentence is on the blackboard, the cat is on the mat at time A. Then, if sentences can be true, the sentence is true: the cat is on the mat. But later, during the same period, the cat flees his mat—say at time B. Then, the sentence will be not true. Since there is one and only one sentence involved, the same sentence will be both true and not true; therefore, it is neither. Moreover, use of the type-token distinction will not enable us to avoid this result, for there is only one sentence token present here.

Since the contradiction is avoidable in other ways, I still do not think that Ziff's arguments are conclusive. We might, for instance, employ what is sometimes described as a "dating device." We might agree that in the above case there is only one sentence persisting through time, but say that it is only a sentence *at a given time* that is either true or false. To say this is to use "sentence" as it is ordinarily used, but it is to change the original claim. Instead of saying that *sentences* are true or false, we now say that *sentences at a given time* are true or false.

Use of a dating device, however, will still not be sufficient. Suppose you and I use the same sentence, "The cat is on the mat," at exactly the same time, but in doing so are referring to different cats. In that case, what you say may be true (since your cat may be on the mat), while what I say may be not true (since my cat may be off his mat). Again, then, the same sentence—and the same sentence used *at the same time*—may be both true and not true. Moreover, there is at least one additional kind of case in which speaking of "true sentences" may lead to contradiction.

Suppose we agree to use the same sentence, at the same time, to refer to the same cat. We both say, for example, "The cat is light," and we say this at the same time, of the same cat. Even so, what you say may be true, while what I say may be false. Suppose that by "light" you mean "not dark" and I mean "not heavy." Now suppose the cat is not dark, but is heavy. In that case, what you have said is true and what I have said is false. Once again, therefore, speaking of "true sentences" will lead to contradiction. We may, of course, be able to avoid such contradictions by introducing some further device, although there will be additional problems caused by the use of certain other linguistic stratagems, such as metaphor, ellipsis, irony, etc. By this time, however, the need to distinguish "sentence" from "statement" has almost vanished, for "sentence" (or "sentence used at a given time," etc.) is being used to mark exactly the same distinctions, or very much the same distinctions, as are ordinarily marked by the use of the term "statement" (or "assertion," etc.). It matters little, then, once "sentence" is used in this new way, whether we say that statements are true or false, or whether we say that sentences are true or false. Only if we do not use "sentence" in this new way—if we use "sentence" only to mean what it ordinarily means—is it important to assert that statements, but not sentences, are either true or false. When I originally made this assertion, I *was* using "sentence" in the ordinary sense, and not in a new, technical sense. I conclude, therefore, that what I originally asserted has been established. Statements, and not sentences, are either true or false.

What emerged in discussing the case of "The cat is light" is this: what is said to be true or false is what the speaker is *saying*. Because two speakers can use the same sentence, even at the same time, to say different things, we cannot identify what is true or false simply with the sentence that the speaker uses. That does not mean that we need identify what is being said only with the *statement* being made. I have already indicated that we can use the term "assertion" here instead of "statement." We might also speak of a "sentence reading" or of a "sentence interpretation." Although finer distinctions can be drawn among these various locutions, there is no need to do so for my purposes. It is sufficient to draw the grosser distinction between what is said and the sentence used to say it. We can then identify "what is said" in various ways: by use of "statement," "assertion," "sentence reading," "sentence interpretation," etc. Of these various alternatives, I shall somewhat arbitrarily use "statement" in preference to the others, and thus identify "what is being said" as the "statement" which the speaker makes and shall describe the statement, in contrast to the sentence, as either true or false.

I should note one further distinction. The phrase "what the speaker said" is itself sometimes used in two distinct ways. In one use of this phrase, I would not be reporting (correctly) what the president said, for example, if I were to use words which the president had not used. This is the sense of "said" used in connection with direct quotation: the president said, "I will fly back to Washington on Tuesday." There is another sense of "said" in which we *would* be reporting (correctly) what the speaker said if we were to offer a correct paraphrase of his remarks. In this second sense, I would be correctly reporting the president's statement if I were to say, "The president said that he would fly back to the Capital tomorrow"—even though I would be using words different from those the president had used. In this second sense of "said," moreover, we can correctly identify what is true or false with what the speaker "said," while in the first sense of "said" we cannot because two speakers can use the same words to make different statements and can use different words to make the same statement. In speaking, then, of what the speaker "said," I shall be using "said" in this second sense to refer not to the exact words of the speaker, but to the statement the speaker makes in using these words.

2

I said earlier that the reasons for our speaking of statements, rather than sentences, as being true or false also demand that we speak of statements, not sentences, as being meaningless or meaningful. I shall now attempt to show that this is so.

At the beginning of the Introduction, I quoted A. J. Ayer as saying that "Stealing money is wrong" is meaningless. Ayer made the claim because he thought that "Stealing money is wrong" is not verifiable (or even confirmable). He did not complain that the *sentence* "Stealing money is wrong" cannot be verified, for such a complaint could be extended to *all* sentences. How, for example, could one possibly verify the sentence "Tom is tall"? The term "Tom" could refer to any Tom whatsoever, and, hence, we would not know which Tom is to have his height checked. The point is that statements, not sentences, are subject to verification, and to argue that a given sentence is meaningless because it cannot be verified is to make a trivial claim. On the same grounds, *all* sentences would be meaningless. Ayer, however, was not making a trivial claim. He was claiming that a particular statement is meaningless.

This can be seen even more clearly by considering the following case. Suppose I say that what I mean in using the term "wrong" is simply "disapproved by people in my society." Now if I say, "Stealing money is wrong," would the Ayer of *Language, Truth and Logic* claim that I had made a meaningless remark? He would not because my remark *can* be verified. We do have ways of checking whether people in my society disapprove of stealing money. If we say, on the other hand, that Ayer denounced the *sentence* "Stealing money is wrong" as meaningless, then we will be forced to say that Ayer would have condemned my remark as meaningless, for I am using the *same* sentence. What Ayer did condemn was the particular statement he thought someone would normally make when using the sentence "Stealing money is wrong." He did not condemn the sentence itself, for the sentence can be used to make various statements, some of which are verifiable and some of which are not.

I think, moreover, that what is true of Ayer's use of the term "meaningless" is true of the usage of nearly all of the philosophers I have cited so far. Using an argument similar to that given above, I think it can be shown that most philosophers who assert that something is meaningless are referring to particular statements, not sentences. That does not prove, of course, that there is nothing wrong with speaking of "meaningless statements," but the burden of proof is shifted, I think, to those who insist that such a way of speaking is defective. Before considering the arguments which purport to prove that this way of speaking is defective, however, I should first like to indicate one consequence of such arguments: that we should give up our philosophical use of the concept of meaninglessness. If "meaningless" is properly predicable of sentences rather than statements, then the use of this notion is of little or no philosophical interest. I shall now show why this is so.

3

Most philosophers who have made assertions of the form "X is meaningless" have meant that X was neither true nor false. I have already indicated that this claim may be too strong. It may be enough to say merely that X could not possibly be true. I shall have more to say on this subject in my final chapter. It is probable, however, that "meaningless" will have to be explained in terms of either "truth" or "falsity," even if not in terms of both. But no sentence, I have already argued, is either true or false. That in itself need not deter us, for we could still explain "meaningless" in terms of "truth" or "falsity," but only at the expense of transforming into trivialities all assertions of the form "X is meaningless."

If we say, as many philosophers have said, that "meaningless" means "neither true nor false," to assert that X is meaningless will be to assert that X is neither true nor false. If X is a sentence, and if *all* sentences fail to be either true or false, then our assertion will be trivial. *All* sentences will be meaningless, and it will be trivial, if not redundant, to assert that any *given* sentence is meaningless. The concept of meaninglessness, then, will be rendered totally sterile.

There is a way, however, to avoid this result, while still applying "meaningless" to sentences. Instead of explaining "meaningless" in terms of either "truth" or "falsity," we might explain it in terms of "capability for making a statement." We might declare, then, that to say that a sentence is meaningless is to say that it cannot be used to make a statement.[3] To say that the sentence "Saturday is in bed" is meaningless, for example, is to say that this sentence cannot be used to make a statement. By taking this route, then, we might predicate "meaningless" of sentences and still avoid the unwanted conclusion that all sentences are meaningless. What I now want to show, however, is that taking this road, as some writers have done, is to head toward still another roadblock—in fact, a total dead-end.

First, a small concession should be made. We might grant, at least for the moment, that there is a class of sentences whose members we might, if we wish, properly describe as "meaningless." Sentences in this class are either grammatically ill-constructed, or they contain one or more meaningless terms (one or more terms which are not words). Take, for example, the following: "The wrong right blue red" and "Snarks have red stripes." The first sentence (assuming that it *is* a sentence) is grammatically incorrect; the second contains a nonsense-term, "snark." We might say, then, that these sentences are meaningless because neither can be used to make a statement. Even in this area, however, there are large obstacles to be overcome. Take, for example, the use of the term "snark." Suppose I say the following: "The term 'snark' has no meaning. Therefore, I do not understand what it means to say that snarks have red stripes." I think that a competent speaker of English would understand what I was saying—that is, the sentences would appear to be meaningful, even though they contain the nonsense term "snark." Thus, not all sentences containing meaningless terms are meaningless.

There is also a problem about our grammatical requirement. Take the grammatically incorrect sentence, "But, if possible, to stimulate someone to

---

[3] In using the term "sentence," I shall be referring *only* to declarative sentences throughout. An interrogative sentence would not be meaningless merely because it could not be used to make a statement.

thoughts of his own." Given a proper setting, however, it can be used to make a statement. For example: "I should not like my writing to spare other people the trouble of thinking. But, if possible, to stimulate someone to thoughts of his own" (Wittgenstein, Introduction to *Philosophical Investigations*). It is quite clear what is being said here; hence, we would not, or at least should not, be tempted to describe the second sentence as "meaningless." We cannot say, therefore, that a sentence is meaningless merely because it is ungrammatical.

I do not think that the obstacles I have raised can be easily circumvented. If they could, and if all of those sentences which are either grammatically incorrect or contain meaningless terms could be correctly described as "meaningless," we would then have a use for "meaningless." We could use it to distinguish between sentences that cannot be used to make a statement (namely, those which either are ill-formed or contain nonsense-terms) and sentences that can. However, almost nothing would have been gained philosophically. For philosophers rarely, if ever, have reason to argue about the meaningfulness of sentences that either are ill-formed or contain nonsense-terms. There is simply seldom any reason to do so. For instance, there is no reason to dispute about the meaningfulness of "The snark has pink stripes" or "The wrong right blue red." The dispute about the propriety of using "meaningless" arose only because some philosophers insisted that certain grammatically correct word-groupings (either sentences or statements) that contained only meaningful terms were nevertheless meaningless. All of the word-groupings cited at the beginning of my Introduction, for example, were of this kind. Thus, even if it could be established that it is correct to speak of a certain class of sentences as meaningless, on the grounds that these sentences could not be used to make statements, it would be of little philosophical interest if the only sentences in that class were those that either were grammatically incorrect or contained nonsense-terms. It would only be of interest if we could say the same of at least some sentences that were both grammatically correct and contained only meaningful terms. It is only in connection with word-groupings of the latter kind that philosophic disputes about meaninglessness have arisen and that the search for adequate criteria of "meaningless" has taken place. When I ask, then, if any sentences are meaningless, I shall henceforth be referring only to sentences which are well constructed and contain meaningful terms: sentences such as "Saturday is in bed."

Are there, then, any meaningless sentences? If there are not, we should renounce the philosophical use of the concept of meaninglessness —assuming, as I am assuming for the moment, that we cannot speak of "meaningless statements," but are forced to speak of "meaningless sentences."

I want to claim that there are no meaningless sentences, for any sentence whatsoever can be used to make a statement. I shall now try to show that this is so. Consider three of the most extreme examples of what have been cited as obvious cases of "meaninglessness":

1. The theory of relativity is blue. (Arthur Pap)
2. Quadruplicity drinks procrastination. (Bertrand Russell)
3. Colorless green ideas sleep furiously. (Noam Chomsky)

Each of these sentences can be used to make statements that could be true. Consider the first sentence in the context of the following situation.[4] An army recruiting sergeant has a file in which he keeps data on various scientific theories. The data on these theories are kept in colored folders. For example, data on the relativity theory is kept in a blue folder and data on quantum theory is kept in a yellow folder. One day, someone comes to the sergeant's office, and asks to look at the file on relativity theory. The sergeant consents, and to help the visitor locate the correct file, he says: "The theory of relativity is blue." In such a situation, the sergeant would not be uttering a meaningless remark, but would be making a true statement. Now consider the second sentence, and a second situation. A play is being given in honor of two nominalist logicians. All of the characters in the play are named after abstractions. For example, one character is named "Virtue" and another is named "Quadruplicity." Even the brands of liquor being served at a party which these characters are attending are named after abstractions. Thus one bottle is labeled "Sloth" and another is labeled "Procrastination." When Quadruplicity is asked what drink he would like, someone else answers in his place: "Quadruplicity drinks procrastination."

The third sentence, "Colorless green ideas sleep furiously," is often

[4] This illustration is borrowed (with changes) from Drange, *Type Crossings,* p. 11.

said to be a particularly extreme case of a meaningless sentence. Yet, even this sentence could, under certain conditions, be used to make a statement. Consider the following dialogue.

A: I feel very disquieted.

B: What is the problem?

A: I think I am being bothered by those green ideas again.

B: Green ideas? I don't understand.

A: You know: those thoughts of envy I spoke to you about. I keep thinking that Mr. C. has something that should be mine.

B: Well, what is it that you want, but don't have?

A: I am not sure yet. It's as if these ideas were asleep in my subconscious, but were tossing and turning in a furious manner.

B: How do you know that something else isn't bothering you?

A: I know I become agitated in this way only when Mr. C. comes to town and I see how well off he is.

B: Well, in the past, which of C's possessions did you think you ought to have?

A: The odd thing is that I have never desired his most exciting possessions, such as his wife or sports car. I only wanted such dull things as his tweed coat and portable typewriter. Perhaps, if these green ideas were not so dull, but were more colorful, I would not be bothered so much. It is the dull, colorless green ideas which lie twisting and turning in my subconscious that really bother me. Colorless green ideas sleep furiously.

By inventing other contexts in this way, we can show that any sentence whatsoever (i.e., any sentence which is well formed and contains only meaningful terms) can be used to make a statement.[5] I have not proved that this is so for all possible sentences, and I do not think that such a proof could be given. It might be possible, therefore, that there is a sentence for which I could not conceive of a context in which the sentence

---

[5] It might be objected here that these are not "normal" contexts. But what is a "normal" context? Finding criteria to distinguish "normal" from "non-normal" contexts would be even more difficult than finding workable criteria for "meaninglessness."

could be used to make a statement. Even if we found such a sentence, it would be rash to assert that no one at all could describe such a context. It would be rasher, still, to say that even given the acquisition of new knowledge which might vastly enrich our imaginations, no one—in any possible age—could conceive of such a context. This would be a particularly bold assertion given the arsenal of linguistic stratagems, including the use of metaphor, ellipsis, irony, etc., at our disposal in trying to describe such contexts. Finally, if necessary, a weaker claim can be made. Even if there are some possible sentences which cannot, in any conceivable contexts, be used to make statements, there are no sentences, or at least not very many, of which this is true that have *so far* appeared in the writings of any leading philosopher. I have not proved even this weaker claim, but I think it could be proved, given sufficient time and space, by simply examining each candidate and showing how it could be used to make a statement in some conceivable context. If either my stronger or weaker claim is true, therefore, we must either give up—as being philosophically uninteresting —the search for adequate criteria of meaninglessness, or we must apply this concept to something other than sentences.

We might still try to avoid the conclusion that "meaningless" has no interesting application, however, without consenting to talk about "meaningless statements." We might substitute for "sentence" some other notion, such as "sentence reading" or "sentence interpretation." Thus, we might speak not of sentences but of "sentence interpretations" as being meaningless. To do this, however, would gain us nothing here. The same arguments which are directed against talk of "meaningless statements" will tell against the use of these other notions as well. Thus, if a *statement* cannot be meaningless, then a *sentence interpretation* or a *sentence reading* cannot be meaningless either. Rather than consider the use of these substitute notions, then, I shall turn directly to the arguments against speaking of "meaningless statements."

To sum up what I have been saying: I have tried to show that if arguments which purport to prove that "meaningless" should apply to sentences rather than statements are conclusive, then we should conclude, not that it is wise to speak of meaningless sentences, but that it is unwise to use the notion of meaninglessness at all. Hence, we should cease all attempts to discover adequate criteria of meaninglessness, for there simply are no meaningless sentences, at least not of the kind that would interest philosophers. Some philosophers, of course, would welcome rather than recoil from this conclusion: for some philosphers suspect that all philosophic talk of meaninglessness is radically misguided and should be stopped instead of encouraged. Before embracing such a conclusion, I think we should carefully examine the arguments which would force its acceptance, to see if these arguments are conclusive. I shall insist that they are not.

4

The standard argument against speaking of "meaningless statements" is quite simple. A statement, so the argument runs, is the meaning of a sentence, or of a class of sentences. We cannot say, then, that a statement is meaningless, for that would amount to saying that a meaning is meaningless and would be self-contradictory. On similar grounds, we cannot say that a statement is meaningful either, for that would be redundant.

A. C. Ewing (using "proposition" to mean what I mean by "statement") expresses this argument as follows:

Note that only sentences can be properly said to have meaning, not propositions. A *proposition is what certain sorts of sentences mean* and cannot again itself have meaning except in a quite different sense of the word, such as that in which the "meaning" of something is equivalent to its implications. A meaningless sentence is a sentence which expresses no proposition.[6] (Italics added)

The defect of this kind of argument is that it assumes that a statement (or proposition) is the meaning of a sentence, or of a group of sentences. Without this assumption, it would not follow that we are asserting that a meaning is meaningless when we assert that a statement is meaningless. But I think that this assumption is false. If a statement were the meaning of a sentence or of a class of sentences, then two or more sentences having the same meaning would express the same statement, for the meaning of these

[6] A. C. Ewing, "Meaninglessness," *Mind*, XLVI (1937), p. 347.

sentences would *be* the statement. But that is not the case. Two sentences can have the same meaning, and, yet, may express different statements. The two sentences "He is a bachelor" and "He is an unmarried man," for example, have the same meaning. Yet, these sentences can be used to express different statements, as when "He" in the first sentence refers to Ludwig Wittgenstein and "He" in the second sentence refers to Bertrand Russell. We cannot say, therefore, that the statements being made are the meanings of the sentences. The statements are different, but the meanings are the same.

If two sentences having the same meaning can be used to express different statements, the converse is also true: two sentences having different meanings can be used to make the same statement. The sentences "He was born in Copenhagen" and "Sören Kierkegaard was born in Copenhagen" do not have the same meaning, for the expressions "He" and "Sören Kierkegaard" are not synonymous. Yet, these two sentences could be used to make the same statement, if, for example, we are referring to the same person when you say, "Sören Kierkegaard was born in Copenhagen," and I say, "He was born in Copenhagen."

There is a further and more obvious reason why a statement cannot be identified with the meaning of a sentence or a class of sentences. Much that is true of statements is obviously not true of meanings. Statements can be true or false; they can also be analytic or synthetic. Meanings can be none of these. It is simply not true, even if it is intelligible, to say that the meaning of my last sentence is true; nor is it true to say that the meaning of my last sentence is false. So, too, statements can be verified or falsified, and meanings cannot. I conclude, then, that it is false to assume that a statement *is* the meaning of a sentence, or of a group of sentences. Since it is false, then the argument which moves from this assumption to the conclusion "that to say that a statement is meaningless is to say that a meaning is meaningless" is unsound. Moreover, similar versions of this same argument, which also make use of this false assumption, are unsound for the same reason.

There is another version of this argument, however, which is slightly different and does not make use of quite the same assumption. Nevertheless, it is unsound for quite similar reasons. Consider, for example, the argument given by John Passmore, who writes:

> Yet, on the whole, the famous distinction of propositions into true, false and meaningless, often regarded—if quite unhistorically—as one of the great glories of twentieth-century philosophy, has been a misfortune. For one thing, these three predicates are not of the same order; true and false are alternative descriptions of statements, of sentences, that is, which are *already known to have a meaning.*[7] (Passmore's italics)

Passmore is not assuming that a statement is the meaning of a sentence. His point, rather, is that a statement is a sentence that already has a meaning. Thus we cannot say that a statement is meaningless, for that would be to say that a sentence which already has a meaning does not have a meaning —which is self-contradictory.

What Passmore *is* assuming, however, is also false. It is false that a statement is a sentence which has a meaning. As I argued earlier, and as Passmore is claiming in this very passage, no sentences are either true or false; it is statements (or assertions, or the like) which are either true or false. If *no* sentences are either true or false, then no sentences already having a meaning are true or false. For example, "the cat is on the mat" already has a meaning, yet, it is neither true nor false. It is the statement, or statements, which could be made by using this sentence that is either true or false. If no sentence already having a meaning is either true or false, and if at least some statements are either true or false, then it is false to assume that statements are sentences already having a meaning. If this assumption is false, then the conclusion does not follow, as Passmore thinks it does, that to assert that a statement is meaningless is to assert that a sentence already having a meaning has no meaning. Such an assertion *would* be self-contradictory (if "meaning" were being used in the same sense in each instance), but the conclusion that this assertion is being made when we speak of meaningless statements is not demonstrated by Passmore's argument. His argument assumes that a statement is a sentence already having a

---

[7] John Passmore, *Philosophical Reasoning* (London: Gerald Duckworth & Co. Ltd., 1963), p. 95.

meaning, and this assumption is false. Statements are not sentences, nor are they the meaning of sentences.

There is a further objection, however, to speaking of meaningless statements. This objection does not depend upon either of the previous assumptions, either that a statement is the meaning of a sentence or that a statement is a sentence which already has a meaning. We might bring out this objection by considering a remark of Wittgenstein's in his *Blue and Brown Books:*

> We don't say that a man who tells us he feels the visual image two inches behind the bridge of his nose is telling a lie or talking nonsense. But we say that we don't understand the meaning of such a phrase. It combines well-known words, but combines them in a way that we don't yet understand. The grammar of this phrase has yet to be explained to us.[8]

Wittgenstein's point is that, although we don't understand what the man is saying, we still do not say that he is speaking nonsense—*because* he might be able to explain his remark. He might go on to explain, for example, that he was using "feel" in a nonliteral sense. Suppose, however, that the man could not, and *logically* could not, explain his remark. If so, we might conclude that his remark was meaningless, but we would also have to conclude that no statement had been made. If a statement had been made, the man could tell us what this statement is, and, hence, could explain his remark. We cannot, therefore, say that a statement had been made and still conclude that the statement is meaningless. I shall now try to show that this objection is untenable.

Suppose you were to say that Saturday is in bed. Very probably, I would not understand your remark. You might, of course, explain that you were referring to a particular man, Mr. Saturday, and saying that he was in bed. In that case, I would understand your remark—what statement you had made. Suppose, however, you were not referring to a man, but were referring, instead, to a day of the week. What, then, would be the situation? I think that you would still be able to explain your remark. If I were

---

[8] Ludwig Wittgenstein, *Blue and Brown Books: Classic Works in Modern Philosophy* (New York: Harper & Row, 1958), p. 10.

puzzled about how you were using the expression "Saturday," you could relieve this puzzlement by saying: "In saying that Saturday is in bed, I was saying that the seventh day of the week is in bed." It is not true, therefore, that you could not explain your remark; and, hence, it need not be true that you had failed to make a statement. When you said that Saturday is in bed, you were asserting that the seventh day of the week is in bed. Furthermore, if I do not understand the expression "seventh day of the week," you could offer an additional paraphrase of your original statement containing a substitute expression that I do understand or could be taught to understand. So, too, if you had been puzzled by the remark about feeling a visual image, the man might have explained that by "feel" he meant "experience." He was claiming, that is, that he experienced a visual image two inches behind the bridge of his nose.

I am not denying that in such cases a man may not be making a statement. Even the words he uses, as opposed to any statement he might make, could be unintelligible. For example, it might be that you were using "Saturday" to refer to neither a person nor a day of the week. In that event, *perhaps* you could not, and logically could not, expain what you had said. If so, then perhaps you had not asserted anything at all. But that does not have to be the case, for once again, you *might* have been making a statement and might have been able to explain to me, by means of paraphrase, what statement you had been making. Moreover, the fact that you could adequately paraphrase your remark is a good indication that you were, in fact, making a statement. I conclude, therefore, that this last objection is not decisive, that meaningless statements, such as "Saturday is in bed," are subject to paraphrase in the same way that other statements are.

I still do not understand, it might be objected, what it would be like for Saturday to be in bed. Telling me that it would be exactly like the seventh day of the week's being in bed will be of no help at all, for I do not understand what that would be like either. Use of paraphrase, therefore, will not, and could not, help me to understand what it would be like for Saturday to be in bed. As William Alson states it: "We simply cannot understand what it would be for Saturday to be in bed (rather than somewhere else) or for two dreams to be comparable in respect of size."[9]

I think that this objection is correct, but it is important to see it clearly. The objection is not that use of paraphrase will fail to help in explaining what statement has been made. If this were the objection, it would be false because I do understand what statement you made. You were asserting, when you said that Saturday is in bed, that the seventh day of the week is in bed. Your paraphrase enabled me to understand that. The objection, then, is something else: even though I now know what statement is being made, I do not understand the statement, for I do not understand what it would be like for Saturday to be in bed. Although I think that this objection is sound, the above may nonetheless be a statement. Consider the self-contradictory statement "Some bachelors are married." We simply cannot understand what it would be like for this statement to be true, for we cannot understand what it would be like for someone to be a bachelor (in the sense I am employing "bachelor" here) while being married. But that is not to say that this statement is not a statement. Self-contradictory statements, although we cannot understand what it would be like for them to be true, are nevertheless statements. So, too, meaningless statements, although we cannot understand what it would be like for them to be true, are nevertheless statements. The objection, therefore, that we cannot understand what it would be like for Saturday to be in bed does not show that we cannot assert it—any more than the analogous objection would prevent our asserting, "Some bachelors are married."

I conclude, then, that we *can* coherently talk of meaningless statements. I have tried to show, moreover, that it is indeed necessary to speak of statements as being meaningless if the concept of meaninglessness is to retain any philosophically important function. Statements rather than sentences should be said to be meaningless for very much the same reasons that statements rather than sentences are either true or false. What is true or false is what a man is saying—that is, what statement he is making—and the same sentence may be used to say quite different things, just as quite different sentences may be used to say the same thing. So, too, what is meaningless or not meaningless is what a man *is* saying—that is, what

[9] William Alston, *Philosophy of Language* (Englewood Cliffs, N.J.: Prentice-Hall, 1964), p. 62.

statement he is making—not what he *might* be saying if he were using his chosen sentence to make some different statement. A man might be saying, for example, that a day of the week is the color of the sky when he uses the sentence "Today is blue Monday"; but if he is merely complaining that today is the day on which he always feels depressed, then what he is saying may not be meaningless—it may, in fact, be true.

There might be an important disanalogy, however, between the attempt to predicate "true" or "false" of sentences and the attempt to predicate "meaningless" of sentences. There are *no* sentences which are either true or false, but there might be sentences that could be correctly described as "meaningless." A sentence which is *radically* defective in terms of grammar, such as "Quickly from what on," might, for example, be said to be "meaningless"—that is, it might be impossible to use this sentence, in any conceivable context, to make a statement.[10] Even if we could use "meaningless" in this way, it would, as I argued earlier, be of little interest to philosophers, for it is of little philosophical interest whether sentences of *this* kind are meaningless. It *would* be interesting, on the other hand, if there were grammatically correct sentences that contained only meaningful terms, and yet were meaningless. But there are no such sentences. If the concept of meaninglessness is to serve any useful philosophic function, therefore, we must be able to speak of certain statements, instead of certain sentences, as being meaningless. I think I have shown that this can be done.

5

I would now like to apply the above results in discussing the radical skepticism I alluded to in my Introduction.

One kind of argument raised in support of radical skepticism is designed to show that what is meaningless is relative to a given language. A

---

[10] As I pointed out earlier, there are obstacles to saying, without qualification, that an ungrammatical sentence is meaningless. Whether there can be said to be meaningless sentences, therefore, would depend upon whether these obstacles can be overcome. One suggested way of avoiding the difficulties is to speak of *radically* ungrammatical sentences (and not simply of ungrammatical sentences *per se*) as being meaningless.

second kind purports to demonstrate that what is meaningless is relative to a particular time. The first kind of argument has been constructed by Karl Popper, and it is his argument that I shall consider first.

Popper begins by claiming that the "doctrine of meaninglessness due to type or category mistakes" was derived from Russell's theory of types. According to Russell's theory, Popper continues, an expression like "A is an element of the class A" must be meaningless; moreover, it must be "essentially" or "inherently" meaningless (by which Popper means "meaningless in all possible languages"). This doctrine, Popper asserts, has long since turned out to be false, for Zermelo and his successors (Fraenkel, Von Neumann, Quine, Ackermann, etc.) have constructed languages in which the expression is well-formed and is thus meaningful. Popper then concludes:

These are, of course, well known facts. But they completely destroy the idea of an 'inherently' or 'naturally' or 'essentially' meaningless expression. For the expression 'A is an element of the class A' turns out to be meaningless in one language but meaningful in another; and this establishes the fact that a proof that an expression is meaningless in some language, must not be mistaken for a proof of intrinsic meaninglessness.[11]

Another similar argument has been employed recently by J. J. C. Smart. After acknowledging his indebtedness to Popper, Smart points out that an expression such as "A is an element of the class A" (the use of which is supposed to generate what is called "Russell's paradox") may be treated in two different ways. It may be said to be meaningless in terms of Russell's type theory, or it may be said to be meaningful if we use Zermelo's set theory. He then concludes:

The possibility of alternative ways of dealing with Russell's paradox has as its analogue alternative ways of dealing with certain controversial sentences: it may be possible to develop science or metaphysics in such a way that they become meaningless, but equally that they may find their place as truths or falsehoods.[12]

[11] See his essay in Schilpp (ed.), *Philosophy of Rudolf Carnap,* p. 195.
[12] J. J. C. Smart, "Nonsense," in *Metaphysics and Explanation,* eds. W. H. Capitan and D. D. Merrill (Oberlin Colloquim in Philosophy, 5th; Pittsburgh: University of Pittsburgh Press, 1966), p. 24.

Popper and Smart, then, are arguing that what is meaningless in a given language may be meaningful, and perhaps true, in some alternative language. If their argument is sound, then this has important, indeed crucial, implications for the use of the concept of meaninglessness. I have yet to say what is being said when we say "X is meaningless," but as I pointed out in my Introduction, the philosophers who have used the concept of meaninglessness have typically tried to prove, in trying to prove that X is meaningless, at least that X could not possibly be true. Most of these philosophers have intended to say that X could not possibly be false either. But the philosophically important claim is that meaningless statements cannot possibly be true—a claim that Popper and Smart are trying to destroy. If they are right, then to say that X is meaningless is merely to say that X is meaningless in a particular language. X may then be significant, and perhaps true, in some other language. Hence, even if we can prove that X is meaningless, that does not prove that X could not possibly be true. Thus, if Popper and Smart are correct, the search for adequate criteria for proving meaninglessness loses most of its philosophical importance. *174468*

Before asking if their argument is sound, however, I should note a prominent unclarity in their conclusion. What kind of language is Popper referring to when he speaks of an expression as being meaningless in one language but meaningful in another? In the case Popper cites, the case of "A is an element of the class A," the language is presumably of a mathematical kind: the expression is meaningless in the language of *Principia Mathematica,* but meaningful in the language of Zermelo's set theory. But what of nonmathematical expressions? Some philosophers have argued that the expression "Brain and mind are identical" is meaningless. What should we say about this expression if we accept Popper and Smart's conclusion? Should we say that if it is meaningless it is meaningless only in English, but it may be meaningful in some other language, say Swedish or Russian? But how could that be? The words "Brain," "and," "mind," "are," and "identical" are all English words. How, then, could the expression "Brain and mind are identical" be part of Swedish or Russian? If it could not, how could it be meaningful in Swedish or Russian? Smart, in contrast to Popper, speaks of "sentences" instead of "expressions." But that fails to help. The sentence "Brain and mind are identical" is a sentence in English, but not a sentence in either Swedish or Russian. Once again, then, how could this same sentence be either meaningful or meaningless in either Swedish or Russian?

I suppose that the words "mind," "and," "brain," "are," and "identical" *could* be used by enough Swedes or Russians so as to become a part of either the Swedish or Russian language. I see no logical difficulty in this supposition. Nevertheless, the likelihood of this occurring seems remote enough to make it questionable whether Popper and Smart are envisioning that. Perhaps what they have in mind, instead, is a change in status of an expression within the *same* language. Thus, "Brain and mind are identical" might be meaningful at a later time, without becoming a non-English expression. The crucial factor, then, would not be a change of languages, but a change of time: what is meaningless *now* may be meaningful *later*.

Other philosophers have made this point about the alleged time-relativity of meaninglessness, but I do not think that Popper and Smart are making it. Rather, I think my first interpretation is correct. To render their conclusion analogous to the claim about the alternative languages of Russell and Zermelo, I think it best to interpret Popper and Smart as concluding that what is meaningless is relative not to a given time but to a given *language* (although, of course, it may also be relative to a given time). What kind of alternative language, however, is unclear. Popper and Smart might be able to explain, of course, what kind of alternative languages they have in mind, and, therefore, I shall not press the question. I do think it worth noting, nevertheless, that their conclusion is not as clear as it might appear to be. (If, on the other hand, I have misinterpreted their conclusion —if Popper and Smart are talking only about the alleged time-relativity of meaninglessness—then part of my argument in this section will be irrelevant. The following section will consider time-relativity.)

Assuming, then, that the conclusion of Popper and Smart is what I have interpreted it to be, I shall argue that it is not supported by their argument. In addition, I shall try to show that no alternative argument could demonstrate their conclusion either.

The premises used by Popper and Smart do not warrant the sweeping conclusion that *any* meaningless statement may be true in some alternative language. Even if some category mistakes were meaningless in one language but meaningful in another, it might be that this phenomenon could occur only with category mistakes. Perhaps other meaningless statements, those that are meaningless because of some defect other than categorial confusion, could not possibly be true in any language whatsoever.

Moreover, it is not true that the development of alternative set theories has shown that category mistakes can be meaningless in one language and meaningful in another. Popper and Smart assume that this result has occurred because they confuse the concept of a category mistake, employed by Gilbert Ryle and others, with the concept of a type mistake, developed by Bertrand Russell and employed in *Principia Mathematica* to dissolve certain kinds of paradoxes. There are affinities between these two concepts, but there are also crucial differences. The most important difference, relative to Popper and Smart's argument, is that one notion applies to statements, the other to sentences. A "category mistake" (in Gilbert Ryle's sense) is a particular statement, such as "Saturday is in bed"; but in Russell's usage, it is a sentence, not a statement, which is said to be a type mistake. For example, the sentence "A is an element of the class A," a type mistake if we use the formation rules of the language of *Principia Mathematica,* is syntactically sound in the language of Zermelo's set theory. Hence, in this latter language, the sentence can be used to make a meaningful statement. That does not show, however, that a category mistake, or any other kind of meaningless statement, was meaningless in one language and is meaningful in another. The most that has been shown is that a sentence of one language may be ill-formed according to the syntax of that language and yet may be well-formed given the syntax of an alternative language.

I think we may conclude, then, that the argument of Popper and Smart does not show that a statement may be meaningless in one language and yet be meaningful in another. Moreover, I do not think that any alternative argument could demonstrate this conclusion. Consider the following.

Let us assume that the statement "Saturday is in bed" is meaningless; perhaps it is a "category mistake," in Ryle's sense of this expression. Suppose, then, that we reformulate the statement in some other language, any language whatsoever. Either the reformulation will have the same meaning or it will not. There is no third alternative. If it does have the same meaning, it will have no meaning, for by hypothesis, "Saturday is in bed" is without meaning. On the other hand, the reformulation may not have the same meaning, in which case it will not be the same statement. Hence, the fact that the reformulation is meaningful will not show that "Saturday is in bed" could be meaningful. Either way, therefore, if a statement such as "Saturday is in bed" is meaningless, reformulating it in some other language will not show that it is meaningful. It will be meaningless no matter what language is used in making it.

Perhaps another way of phrasing this last conclusion is the following. Statements, unlike sentences, are not *in* languages; they do not belong, that is, to any one language. For example, I may use English words to state that today is Saturday; or I may use words of some other language, such as French or Italian, to state the same thing. Regardless of which language I speak, there is only one statement to be made here, not three (or more) different statements. If statements are not in any given language, then it is not true—it is not even coherent—to say that a statement may be meaningless in one language and meaningful in another. Thus, if my statement that today is Saturday is meaningful, then speaking French or Italian or any other language will not change the matter. The same logic applies to meaningless statements.

6

I tried to show in the preceding section that the argument concerning the alleged language-relativity of meaninglessness is unsound. I shall now consider a different argument: that what is meaningless is relative to a given time. What may be meaningless now, given the existing state of our knowledge, may be meaningful tomorrow, when we acquire new knowledge. Both Hilary Putnam and Paul Ziff seem to make this claim, and I think that other philosophers would agree with such a claim.

Putnam presents his argument in discussing Max Black's claim that the so-called "identity" thesis is meaningless. He writes:

Consider the sentence (1) **Pain** is identical with stimulation of C-fibers.

The sentence is deviant (so the argument runs, though not in this terminology): there is no statement that it could be used to make in a normal context. Therefore, if a philosopher advances it as a thesis he must be giving the words a new meaning, rather than expressing any sort of discovery. For example, (Max Black argued) one might begin to say 'I have stimulated C-fibers' instead of 'I have a pain,' etc. But then one would *merely* be giving the expression 'has stimulated C-fibers' the new meaning 'is in pain.' The contention is that as long as the words keep their present meanings, (1) is unintelligible.

I agree that the sentence (1) is a 'deviant' sentence in present-day English. I do *not* agree that (1) can never become a normal, non-deviant sentence unless the words change their present meanings.

The point, in a nutshell, is that what is 'deviant' depends very much upon context, including the state of our knowledge, and with the development of new scientific theories it is constantly occurring that sentences that did not previously 'have a use,' that were previously 'deviant,' acquire a use —not because the words acquire *new* meanings, but because the old meanings as fixed by the core of stock uses, *determine* a new use given the new context.[13]

I think that Putnam's argument is unsound *if* interpreted as an attempt to show that what is meaningless now may be meaningful tomorrow. I may be unfair in interpreting Putnam's argument in this way; however, his reference to Max Black, and his later reference in the same article to Norman Malcolm's discussion of the concept of dreaming, lead me to believe that my interpretation is fair. Both Black and Malcolm were arguing that a certain thesis could not possibly be true *because* it was *meaningless;* and it is *their* arguments that Putnam claims to be discussing (although, by his own admission, in a different terminology). I think, then, that Putnam *is* trying to defend the thesis that what is meaningless today may be meaningful tomorrow.

The first defect of Putnam's argument concerns the shift in terminology which Putnam mentions. Putnam's opponent, Max Black, employed

[13] Hilary Putnam, "Minds and Machines," in *Dimensions of Mind,* ed. Sidney Hook (New York: New York University Press, 1960), p. 166.

the concept of meaninglessness, not the notion of "logical deviance." This point by itself is crucial, for the notion of "deviance," which Putnam borrows from Paul Ziff (after explicitly acknowledging his indebtedness), is not the same as meaninglessness. To say that a given sentence is "deviant" is to say no more, as Putnam and Ziff employ the concept, than that its use would be a departure from an empirical regularity. For example, to say, "Pass the mustard" when no mustard is present is to make a "deviant" utterance. It is easy to see, then, why what is deviant today may not be deviant tomorrow: the relevant empirical regularity may change at some later time. The term "deviance," moreover, unlike the term "meaningless," should not be used as a term of criticism at all.[14]

It is true, then, that what is deviant today may be nondeviant tomorrow. Given Ziff's definition of "deviance," it is quite *obviously* true and not something which Max Black would deny. He would deny, I take it, that the identity thesis to which Putnam referred could be both meaningless today and meaningful tomorrow, and Putnam's argument about "deviance" in no way shows that Black's denial would be incorrect. To argue, as Putnam does, that what is deviant can also be nondeviant is not to argue that what is meaningless could also be meaningful. The two concepts are not the same.

There is a second defect in Putnam's argument. Instead of discussing the identity *thesis,* which is a particular *statement* about the alleged identity of mind and brain, he discusses a particular *sentence*. Now I agree with Putnam that the particular sentence, "Pain is identical with stimulation of C-fibers," could be used in the future to make a statement in some "normal" context. It might be possible even if no such "normal" context presently existed. That in no way shows that a particular *statement,* which this sentence has been used to make, could be meaningless now and meaningful later; and it is a certain statement, not a sentence which might be used to make an unknown statement at an unknown date, that constitutes the identity thesis. Hence, to argue, as Putnam does, that the sentence used in stating this thesis might be used to make a statement in some "normal" context at some later date is not to argue that the identity thesis

[14] Ziff, *Semantic Analysis,* p. 122.

104

could be meaningful. I might try to show, for example, that "the seventh day of the week sleeps in a bed" is a thesis that could be meaningless now and meaningful later by arguing that the sentence "Saturday is in bed" could be used to make a statement in some "normal" context at some future date, if someone were to use these words when referring to a Mr. Saturday. Such an argument, however, would be transparently irrelevant. In the same way, Putnam's argument about the possible use of the sentence "Pain is identical with stimulation of C-fibers" is also irrelevant to the question whether the identity thesis could be meaningless at one time and meaningful at a later time.

Paul Ziff's argument is quite similar to Putnam's argument and suffers from the same two defects. Ziff writes:

> 'At exactly what moment during the time that he was sound asleep did the dream occur?', 'Does time bend back on itself?', 'There are infinitely many stars': perhaps for the time being these are deviant utterances. But just wait: what could not be said yesterday is the idiom of today. We cannot say what will be said tomorrow.[15]

Both objections I made earlier apply here; and neither needs to be stated in much detail. It is quite true that the idiom of today might have been deviant yesterday. As Putnam points out, it was deviant yesterday, at least before the invention of writing, to say, "I am a thousand miles away from you."[16] Although saying this would have been deviant, it still could have been said. The utterance was deviant but not meaningless. Further, as Ziff uses "utterance"—which he explicitly distinguishes from "statement"[17]—I might make the same utterance at different times and yet make two different statements, just as I might use the same sentence at different times to make two different statements. For example, I might be able to utter the words "There are infinitely many stars" on two occasions and make two different statements. It could happen that, in uttering the same words both today and tomorrow, I might make a meaningless statement today and a meaningful statement tomorrow, simply because the two statements might be different. But this in no way shows that the *same statement* could be both meaning-

---

[15] *Ibid.*, p. 197.
[16] Putnam, "Minds and Machines," p. 167.
[17] Ziff, *Semantic Analysis*, p. 120.

less today and meaningful tomorrow. Ziff's argument, like Putnam's, is quite irrelevant to the question whether the *same statement* can be meaningless at one time and meaningful later.

I am not claiming, however, that the arguments of Putnam and Ziff misfire completely. I do think that at least some philosophers have argued that a given *sentence* is meaningless merely because there is no context in which it could be used to make a statement. Insofar as certain philosophers have done this, then I think that it is relevant to argue, as Putnam and Ziff do, that although this may be true of a given sentence today, it may be false tomorrow. But there are other philosophers against whom Putnam and Ziff are arguing—for example, those philosophers who claim that the identity thesis is meaningless. To confute these other philosophers, in the way in which Putnam and Ziff intend, it must be shown that a given *statement* could be both meaningless now and meaningful later. What I am claiming, however, is that the arguments of Putnam and Ziff both fail to show this; both arguments are irrelevant to this second issue.

chapter v

metaphors and meaninglessness

There are certain interesting connections between the use of metaphor and the use of the concept of meaninglessness. I shall try to bring out some of these connections by examining certain philosophic views of the nature of metaphor and by showing how these views lead to skepticism concerning either the employment of metaphor or the use of the concept of meaninglessness.[1]

1

Two views of metaphor are especially relevant here. According to the first and older view, all metaphors are meaningless. According to the second and more sophisticated view, there is nothing wrong with the use of metaphor, but there is something wrong with the use of the concept of meaninglessness because it forces us to say that metaphors are meaningless.

The first view of metaphor may be accepted for various reasons. One reason, for example, for saying that metaphors are meaningless is based on the definition of the concept of metaphor in terms of the concept of a category mistake. Colin Turbayne, for instance, defines the notion of

---

[1] Some writers see the use of metaphor as presenting a major obstacle to the use of the concept of meaninglessness. For example, R. Routley, although he believes the obstacle can be circumvented, writes: "One problem which threatens to destroy a significance theory before it begins is the problem of metaphor and transference of sense." See "On a Significance Theory," *Australasian Journal of Philosophy*, XLIV (1966), p. 178.

metaphor in this way in his interesting book, *The Myth of Metaphor*. He writes:

> Gilbert Ryle offers a still better definition of metaphor: 'It represents the facts . . . *as if* they belonged to one logical type or categories, when they actually belong to another.' This greatly illuminates the subject of metaphor because it draws our attention to those two features that I have been stressing, namely sort-crossing or the fusion of different sorts, and the pretense or *as if* feature. I should again point out, however, that although this definition is about the best definition of metaphor known to me, it is not Ryle's definition of metaphor at all. It is, indeed, his alternative definition of category-mistake or categorial confusion.[2]

It would seem, given the above definition of "metaphor," that every metaphor is an instance of categorial confusion. Turbayne, however, subsequently balks at this implication and denies that all metaphors are mistakes. He is unclear, however, about what gives him the right to deny this implication once he has accepted the above definition. At one point, he seems to think that he is justified because it need not be a mistake to cross types. Thus he writes: "But it seems altogether unlikely that Ryle regards metaphors as mistakes, for such 'category mistakes' may have great value. It is not necessarily a mistake to cross sorts."[3] He then goes on to point out that it is only a mistake when one crosses sorts or types "without awareness,"—that is, when one takes a metaphor literally.[4] Still later, however, he writes in a way that rules out anyone's ever taking a metaphor literally:

> But since metaphor is not a metaphor *per se* but only for someone, from one point of view it is better to say that sometimes the metaphor is not noticed; it is hidden. That is, if X is aware of the metaphor while Y is not, X says that Y is being taken in by the metaphor, or being used by it, or taking it literally. But for Y it is not a case of taking the metaphor literally at all, because for him there is no metaphor. He is speaking literally or taking it literally.[5]

According to Turbayne's account, then, all metaphors, by definition, are category mistakes; but not all category mistakes, or type crossings, are

---

[2] Colin Turbayne, *The Myth of Metaphor* (New Haven: Yale University Press, 1962), p. 17.
[3] *Ibid.*, p. 22.
[4] *Ibid.*
[5] *Ibid.*, p. 23.

mistakes. Category mistakes are only mistakes when taken literally. Thus, although all metaphors are category mistakes, only metaphors which are taken literally are mistakes. Since, however, metaphors are not metaphors *per se,* but only from a given point of view, *no* metaphor can possibly be taken literally: if it is taken literally, it is not a metaphor.

I think that this part of Turbayne's account is confused. Rather than try to straighten out his analysis, I shall simply expose what I believe to be the initial mistake which causes the confusion: the attempt to define "metaphor" in terms of "category mistake." However, I should first mention another reason for viewing metaphors as meaningless—one discussed by Elizabeth Hungerland in her *Poetic Discourse.* She writes:

> For a time, linguistic meaning resided exclusively with cognition. How, some philosophers asked, could a sentence be meaningful unless it were verifiable? 'Life is a tale told by an idiot' is hardly the kind of sentence that reports facts, describes things—it cannot be either true or false; it is accordingly meaningless. (The philosophers in question did not, of course, deny that poetry has human and rhetorical significance, but they failed to find meaning 'in the strict linguistic sense' in much of poetic discourse.)[6]

Mrs. Hungerland is referring, of course, to the logical positivists. If they accepted this view of metaphor, it was because they also accepted a verificationist view of meaning; however, it is not clear that the positivists did hold this view. Mrs. Hungerland does not name a particular positivist. Indeed, it is difficult to find an explicit statement by any leading positivist that all metaphors are meaningless, although such a view is perhaps suggested by Carnap when he writes:

> The aim of a lyrical poem in which occur the words 'sunshine' and 'clouds,' is not to inform us of certain meteorological facts, but to express certain feelings of the poet and to excite similar feelings in us. A lyrical poem has no assertional sense, no theoretical sense, it does not contain knowledge.[7]

Since "no theoretical sense," for Carnap, is equivalent to "cognitively meaningless," it would seem to follow that lyrical poetry is meaningless, or

---

[6] *Poetic Discourse* (Berkeley, Calif.: University of California Press, 1958), p. 1.
[7] Rudolf Carnap, "The Rejection of Metaphysics," in *Age of Analysis,* ed. Morton White (New York: Mentor Books, 1955), p. 219.

cognitively meaningless. It is not clear whether Carnap wants to describe all poetry in this way, and, if so, whether he wishes to describe as meaningless all uses of metaphor, or only uses of metaphor within poetry.[8]

Perhaps the most explicit statement of this "positivist" view of poetry, assuming that it was the view of the positivists, is to be found in the writings not of a philosopher but of the poet Archibald MacLeish, who concludes his poem "Ars Poetica" with the lines:

> A poem should be equal to:
> Not true
> For all the history of grief
> An empty doorway and a maple leaf
> For love
> The leaning grasses and two lights above the sea—
> A poem should not mean
> But be

Even if the positivists did hold the view that all metaphors are meaningless, however, I doubt that many philosophers writing today, even among contemporary positivists, would accept such a view. In fact, there is a contrary view which, I think, would find more favor today among many philosophers. According to this contrary view, poetic uses of language are quite respectable; what is not respectable is the use of the concept of meaninglessness. Suppose, for example, we say that "He had a green thought" is nonsensical. Now suppose we find this sentence, or one very much like it, appearing in a poetic context. We should not say that the poet was speaking nonsense; therefore, we should not say that "He had a green thought" is nonsensical in the first place. Thus Paul Ziff writes:

> I shall not discuss whether or not 'He had a green thought' is nonsensical. However, I can see not the slightest reason to suppose that it is nonsensical. When Andrew Marvell wrote 'Annihilating all that's made to a green thought in a green shade' he was not making a mistake, neither did he write anything nonsensical.[9]

[8] He does go on to say that "all arts have this non-theoretical character," which does suggest that he is talking about all poetry and not just lyrical poetry.

[9] Paul Ziff, "About Ungrammaticalness," *Mind* (1964), p. 210. A similar view is hinted at in the following comment by A. C. Baier: "What one philosopher will classify as senseless—for example, 'Virtue is green'—another will class as false, and the literary critic may well find the same words in a suitably enriching context, illuminating and apt." See his article "Nonsense" in *The Encyclopedia of Philosophy*, ed. Paul Edwards (vol. V; New York: The Macmillan Company, 1967).

I shall now try to show that both of the views outlined above are mistaken and that they are mistaken for the same reason.

Take, first, the view that all metaphors are meaningless. We might be tempted to say this either because we accept a verificationist criterion of meaninglessness or because we accept a category or type criterion. Regardless of which criterion we are employing, however, and irrespective of whether such a criterion is reliable, we should resist this temptation. Even if it is true that a meaningless statement would be made if a sentence were being used literally—or if one or more of the words within the sentence were being used literally—it fails to follow that the statement made when the sentence is being used metaphorically is also meaningless. The statements made are not the same: using a group of words literally and then metaphorically will result in two different statements.[10] Suppose, for example, I assert that "There will be a time when logics die." Moreover, I explain that by "logics" I mean "formal systems" and that the rest of my words are also to be interpreted literally. In that case, we might say that my statement is meaningless and that, perhaps, a category mistake has been committed. A formal system is not the kind of thing one could describe as "dying," at least not in a literal sense. Or, to take a second example, I might be accused of uttering nonsense if I speak of "thoughts that smell in the rain"—a charge that might be justified, if I am speaking literally.

Suppose, instead, that these words are not to be taken literally. Dylan Thomas, for example, speaks in one of his poems of "thoughts that smell in the rain"; he also writes of a time "when logics die." Thomas, presumably, is speaking metaphorically. In using the term "logics," for example, he does not mean "formal systems": he is not asserting that formal systems die. Thomas is not making the same statements, therefore, that I made earlier; and, hence, we need not say that his statements are meaningless merely because mine were.

Because a category mistake is a particular *statement,* not a sentence, it is wrong to define "metaphor" in terms of "category mistake." Thus, even if using a given sentence literally would produce a category mistake, using the same sentence metaphorically would not. The most we can say, it

---

[10] I shall speak throughout of a *sentence* being used metaphorically, even though it may be more apt to speak only of a word, or a group of words, within the sentence as being so used.

seems, is that metaphors would be category mistakes, or at least meaning-less, *if* they were read literally. But we cannot even say that. Consider the following lines from W. H. Auden's poem "In Memory of W. B. Yeats," written in January of 1939:

> In the nightmare of the dark
> All the dogs of Europe bark,
> And the living nations wait
> Each sequestered in its hate.

In the first two lines, Auden is referring not to yelping canines but to quarreling nations: he is not claiming that, on some night in January of 1939, all of the canines in Europe were yelping and growling. Instead, he is saying, roughly, that in the ominous days which preceded the outbreak of World War II, the nations of Europe were quarreling like barking dogs. Suppose, however, we interpret Auden literally. Suppose we understand him as saying that, on some given night in January of 1939, all the canines in Europe were barking. His assertion might then be false, for perhaps there was no such night in January of 1939. Although false, however, such an assertion would not be nonsensical. It is not even true, then, that all metaphors are nonsensical if read literally. Nevertheless, the important point is that metaphors are not meant to be read literally. Even if it *were* true that all metaphors are meaningless if interpreted literally, it would still not follow that all metaphors are meaningless. If a speaker is using words metaphorically, he is not speaking literally. Hence, he is not making the meaningless statement he would be making if he were speaking literally. It is wrong, then, to say that all metaphors are meaningless.

It is also wrong to conclude that use of the concept of meaninglessness is suspect merely because the use of metaphors is not. Suppose, for example, that it is meaningless to assert literally that "He had a green thought." That does not imply that if a poet uses these same words metaphorically, he, too, is uttering nonsense or making a mistake of some kind. The poet, if he is making an assertion at all, is not making the same assertion made when these words are used literally. He may be using the same sentence, but he is not making the same statement.

Both of the above views, then, are incorrect because they fail to distinguish between the metaphor and the sentence used in stating the metaphor. The sentence "He had a green thought" may be used literally to make a meaningless statement; but it may also be used metaphorically to make a different statement, which is not meaningless. We need not conclude, therefore, that all metaphors are meaningless; but neither must we conclude, merely because at least some metaphors are not meaningless, that there is something illegitimate or suspicious about the use of the concept of meaninglessness.

2

I have said that in using a sentence metaphorically we are not making the same statement which would be made if the sentence were used literally. We are making a different statement. What is this "different" statement? Is *it* meaningful? If it is not, then we shall still be forced to conclude that all metaphors are meaningless, even after distinguishing the metaphor and the sentence used in stating the metaphor.

According to one very widely held view of metaphor, this "different" statement is simply a simile—a statement making a literal comparison between two terms. This view, which is often referred to as the "comparison view" of metaphor, is described by a leading literary critic, Northrop Frye, in his work *The Anatomy of Criticism.* He writes:

> Descriptively, then, all metaphors are similes. When we are writing ordinary discursive prose and use a metaphor, we are not asserting that A is B: we are 'really' saying that A is in some respects comparable with B; and similarly when we are extracting the descriptive or paraphrasable meaning of a poem. 'The hero was a lion,' then, on the descriptive level, is a simile with the word 'like' omitted for greater vividness, and to show more clearly that the analogy is only a hypothetical one.[11]

If this view is correct, there is no problem about the meaningfulness of the statement that is "really" made when we speak metaphorically. The statement that is "really" made is not the nonsensical statement which (in many cases) would be made if the sentence were being used literally; instead, it is

[11] Northrop Frye, *The Anatomy of Criticism* (Princeton, N.J.: Princeton University Press, 1957), p. 123.

a straightforward statement making a comparison between two terms. There is no reason why this comparison statement would have to be meaningless. There is no reason, for example, to conclude that a statement such as "Richard is like a lion" is meaningless. If we accept this comparison analysis, therefore, we can avoid the conclusion that all metaphors are meaningless.

Recently, however, the comparison analysis of metaphor has been challenged as being inadequate. Max Black, for example, has argued, in a recent and highly influential article, that the comparison analysis has to be supplemented, at least for a certain class of cases, by what he terms an "interaction" analysis.[12] According to the interaction view of metaphor, a metaphor "works" by having the predicate-term interact with the subject-term, thus causing a change in meaning of the subject-term. To use Black's example, saying that "Man is a wolf" changes the meaning of the term "man," for after using the metaphor, man seems more wolf-like—more predatory, voracious, treacherous, etc. It is because of this shift in meaning, moreover, that the comparison view is said to be inadequate. If we translate the wolf-metaphor as "Man is like a wolf (in some respects)," we are using the term "man" here in its old sense, and "man" does not now have this sense.

Recently, Black's analysis has been employed by certain philosophers of science in their discussion of scientific theories. Mary Hesse, who claims that scientific theories should be viewed as metaphors, argues that Black's analysis is incompatible with assumptions generally made in the "deductive account" of scientific explanation. In the deductive account, Miss Hesse points out, terms appearing in scientific laws are assumed to remain invariant in meaning to all changes of explanatory theory. For example, the term "mass" would have the same meaning in different theories. But if expanatory theory functions as a metaphor, and if in metaphorical description the meanings of terms do not remain invariant, the deductive account, Miss Hesse argues, has to be modified. She writes:

Men are seen to be more like wolves after the wolf-metaphor is used, and wolves seem more human. Nature becomes more like a machine in the

[12] Max Black, *Models and Metaphors* (Ithaca, N.Y.: Cornell University Press, 1962).

mechanical philosophy, and actual, concrete machines themselves are seen as if stripped down to their essential qualities of mass in motion.

This point is the kernel of the interaction view, and is Black's major contribution to the analysis of metaphor. It is incompatible with the comparison view, which assumes that the literal descriptions of both systems are and remain independent of the use of the metaphor, and the metaphor is reducible to them. The consequences of the interaction view for theoretical models are also incompatible with assumptions generally made in the deductive account of explanation, namely that descriptions and descriptive laws in the domain of the explanandum remain empirically acceptable and invariant in meaning to all changes of explanatory theory.[13]

I shall now examine what Miss Hesse says here, without attempting to cover all of the interesting points she raises about the connection between theories and metaphors. I shall also disregard her assertion that the interaction analysis is *incompatible* with the comparison analysis. Black does not make such a claim; he claims only that the interaction analysis is needed as a *supplement* to cover a certain class of cases for which the comparison analysis seems inadequate. In some cases, at least, the comparison analysis would be sufficient. To bring Miss Hesse's view in line with Black's, therefore, I shall assume that she is making only the weaker claim that an interaction analysis is required not to rival but to supplement the comparison analysis.

The reason the comparison analysis is inadequate, according to Black and Hesse, is that use of a metaphor results in a change in meaning of the subject-terms (and perhaps of the predicate-term as well). It is this change in meaning that allegedly prevents our paraphrasing metaphors in the manner suggested by the comparison analysis. I should now like to suggest, however, that we have a right to be skeptical about this "change in meaning" claim.

To use an example which both Black and Hesse use—one for which the interaction analysis is supposedly required—need a change in meaning occur in the term "man" merely because the wolf-metaphor has been used? I doubt that this is so. Suppose, for example, that I have just learned of my

[13] Mary Hesse, "The Explanatory Function of Metaphor," in *Logic, Methodology and Philosophy of Science*, ed. Y. Bar-Hillel (Amsterdam: North-Holland Publishing Co., 1965), p. 252.

dismissal from my university post and that I suspect my colleagues of having voted for my dismissal only because they seek to gain from my departure. Disgruntled and disenchanted, I might utter to myself, "Man is a wolf." Suppose, however, that no one—neither I nor anyone else—ever utters these words again. It seems implausible that the meaning of "man" would have changed simply because a single speaker used the wolf-metaphor on one occasion. If no one heard me utter the words "Man is a wolf," then how will *my* single use of this metaphor affect the usage of *other* speakers? If my use of the metaphor has no effect on how other speakers use the term "man," then how will the meaning of the term "man," as this term is used by other speakers, be altered? The most that would result would be that the meaning of "man" as *it is used in the ideolect of a single speaker* would change. But now I want to argue that even this is implausible. Suppose I later learn that the news of my dismissal had been a mistake, and suppose that I completely forget my feeling of disenchantment with my colleagues. Might I not then view man in the same manner as before and use the term "man" in the very same ways as before? If such were the case, how would the meaning of the term "man" have changed even for me?

Suppose that others were to use the wolf-metaphor as well. This has, in fact, happened. Since Black's article was written (in 1954), and even prior to that time, the wolf-metaphor has been used, if only as an illustration, on numerous occasions. Has this resulted in a change of meaning of the term "man"? I think this, too, is implausible. It is not altogether clear what it means to say that a term has "changed its meaning"; hence, it is not altogether clear what it means to deny such an assertion.[14] I do think, however, that there are some things we can say about "change in meaning." For example, I think it can be said that a term has *not* changed in meaning when used in making two separate statements, if a statement containing the term is *inconsistent* with a subsequent statement which contains the same term and is the apparent denial of the original statement. For example, if I say at time T_1, "Philosophy is dull," and at time T_2, "Philosophy is not

---

[14] For useful discussions of the topic, see: Peter Achinstein, *Concepts of Science* (Baltimore: The Johns Hopkins Press, 1968), esp. pp. 91–105; and Dudley Shapere, "Meaning and Scientific Change," in *Mind and Cosmos,* ed. R. Colodny (Pittsburgh: University of Pittsburgh Press, 1966), pp. 41–85.

dull"—and if my statements are inconsistent—then the meaning of the term "philosophy" is the same in both statements. If the meaning of the term "philosophy" (or of the other terms) were not the same, the statements would not be inconsistent.

Let us apply this test to the case of "man." Suppose that Max Black was the first person to use the wolf-metaphor and that he used it for the first time in 1954. Has the meaning of the term "man" changed since that time? I doubt that it has. If Black had said prior to 1954, "All men must die," and if he, or any other employer of the wolf-metaphor, were now to say, "Not all men must die," would not the second statement be inconsistent with the first? If so, would this not show that the meaning of the term "man" had *not* changed? Either Black or Miss Hesse might wish to claim, however, that these statements were *not* inconsistent, but only seemed to be. They would, then, have to provide some argument to support their claim. Until such an argument is provided, I think we are justified in being skeptical of the claim that the meaning of the term "man" has changed; therefore, we should in turn be skeptical of the thesis that using a metaphor changes the meaning of one or more of its component terms. This is not to say, however, that use of a metaphor *never* results in a change in meaning. I do think that repeated and constant use of a metaphor sometimes does cause a change in meaning, as when a live metaphor becomes a dead metaphor. Of the two illustrations used by Miss Hesse, a more plausible argument might be made for saying that the second is a dead metaphor and that the term "nature" has changed in meaning as a result of the repeated use of the "machine" metaphor. Now, I want to argue that even when a change of meaning does occur, the change will not affect our ability to paraphrase the metaphor in the manner suggested by the comparison analysis.

Let us assume that the term "nature" has changed in meaning and that the change has occurred because of extensive use of the "machine" metaphor. Suppose, then, that "nature" means something different at times T_1 and T_2—where T_1 is a time during Newton's lifetime, and T_2 is a time after 1800. If someone were to say at time T_1 that "Nature is a machine," he would not have been speaking both literally and truly. At time T_1 it was not literally true to say that "Nature is a machine." The speaker, of course, might have been speaking metaphorically, depending, in part, on his intentions. In that case, we could have interpreted the speaker, as the comparison analysis suggests, as saying that nature is *like* a machine (in certain respects).

Suppose, however, that after constant use of this metaphor the term "nature" developed a new sense. Using "nature" in this new sense, then, it would be literally true to say, "Nature is a machine." Hence, if someone were to use this sentence at time T_2, a time after which "nature" had developed this second sense, he could be speaking literally and yet be making a true statement. The comparison analysis would then be *inappropriate,* for the speaker would not be saying that "nature is *like* a machine"; he would be saying, literally and truly, that "Nature *is* a machine." If the comparison analysis is inappropriate here, that does not mean that some other analysis, such as the interaction analysis, is needed. *No* metaphoric analysis is needed, simply because the speaker at time T_2 would not be speaking metaphorically at all. He would be speaking both literally and truly. Even where use of a metaphor does result in a change in meaning, therefore, no additional analysis is needed to supplement the comparison analysis. Thus, it would have been necessary at time T_1 to interpret "Nature is a machine" metaphorically; but at time T_2, no such need would have been present. This should not seem particularly puzzling, however, once we have distinguished sentences from statements. Although the same sentence would be used at both times, the statements made by the *literal* use of the sentence would be different at each of the two times. It is not surprising, then, that the statement made at T_1 by the literal use of "Nature is a machine" would be nonsensical or obviously false, while the statement made at T_2 by the literal use of this same sentence would be true: the two statements would be different.

What allows the speaker to use the same sentence to make a different statement at different times is that one of the terms in the sentence has developed a new sense in the interim between the two uses; i.e., enough speakers have used the term in this novel way on enough occasions to warrant our saying that the term now has two literal senses, whereas before it had only one. The term "fork," for example, now has a second literal sense which it lacked at an earlier time. At one time, "fork" meant only "eating utensil." Through constant use of the metaphor "There is a fork in the road," however, the term developed a second sense, namely "branch" or "break." As a result, we can now make literal use of the sentence "There is a fork in the road" and make a different statement from that which would have been made had this same sentence been used literally before the development of the second sense. This phenomenon of the same sentence being used to make two different statements can occur in cases where metaphor is not involved at all—where, for example, someone merely stipulates that he will use a term in a new technical sense. I conclude, therefore, that the change in meaning *sometimes* brought about by the extensive use of a metaphor—a change in which a live metaphor becomes a dead metaphor—presents no special problem concerning the analysis of metaphor; that is, no problem which is either peculiar to the use of metaphor, or which cannot be handled by the comparison analysis of metaphor. I do not think, therefore, that the "special" analysis—the interaction analysis suggested by Max Black and Mary Hesse—is either a successful rival of, or a useful supplement to, the comparison analysis described earlier.

Perhaps the truth of Black's and Hesse's assertions comes to this: in many cases, especially in the case of a strikingly good metaphor, no paraphrase will be entirely acceptable. No matter what we might suggest as a paraphrase, we are inclined to say that something is left out, that the metaphor does not mean *exactly* that. T. E. Hulme, for example, asks of the line from Keats' "Isabella," "And she forgot the blue above the trees":

Why did he put 'blue above the trees' and not 'sky'? 'Sky' is just as attractive an expression. . . . Simply for this reason, that he instinctively felt that the word 'sky' would not convey over the actual vividness and the actuality of the feelings he wanted to express.[15]

We could paraphrase Keats' remark by substituting "sky" for "blue," but the paraphrase would not be quite right: Keats did not mean exactly that. In such a case, where no exact paraphrase can be found, the comparison analysis will seem unacceptable, although not because, as suggested by

[15] Quoted by John Hospers in *Meaning and Truth in the Arts* (Chapel Hill: The University of North Carolina Press, 1946), p.178.

Black and Hesse, use of the metaphor changes the meaning of one or more of the key terms in the sentence. As I have already argued, the use of any metaphor may fail to cause a change in meaning; and if a change in meaning does occur, that will not in itself affect our ability to paraphrase the metaphor. Moreover, the difficulty of finding exact paraphrases does not arise only in cases of metaphor. In speaking literally, if a speaker uses his words skillfully and precisely, an exact paraphrase may not be available. No paraphrase of even some of the literal passages of Lincoln's "Gettysburg Address," for example, will serve quite as well as the original. "Four-score and seven years ago, our fathers brought forth upon this continent a new nation" may mean *roughly* the same as "Eighty-seven years ago, our ancestors founded a new country in North America," but the second statement does not have exactly the same meaning as the first.

I would now like to suggest why exact paraphrases are very often not available. This reason has nothing to do with "change in meaning" and, in fact, has no essential connection with metaphors. The reason is simply that there are very few cases of synonyms, or synonymous phrases, being exactly equivalent in meaning. In the case of almost every pair of synonyms, there are some conceivable contexts in which one of the terms could not replace the other without altering the meaning of what was said. Take, for example, the terms "statement" and "assertion." The second of these terms is often used, and rightly so, as a synonym for the first. Thus, if I were to say, "Maxwell's statement about the ether later proved to be false," someone might correctly paraphrase this as, "Maxwell's assertion about the ether later proved to be false." It is easy to show, however, as Paul Ziff does, that "statement" and "assertion" are not *exactly* synonymous.[16] One may be making a statement, for example, in saying, "I suppose things have gotten a bit out of hand," but one is not making an assertion. So, too, to say, "The President made a statement to the press," is not to say, "The President made an assertion to the press."

That there are few pairs of synonyms exactly equivalent in meaning often makes finding *exact* paraphrases difficult. If one group of words is substituted for another, we can often point to *some* difference in meaning

[16] Ziff, *Semantic Analysis,* p. 120.

between the two groups, no matter how slight, by pointing to some possible context in which one of the terms in the new group will not mean the same as the corresponding term, or set of terms, in the former group. In some cases, the difference in meaning will be so slight as to be unnoticeable, but in many cases it will not. In the latter kind of case, a paraphrase may seem unacceptable. Such a case may be a case of metaphor. Often it is, but sometimes it is not.

To sum up: I agree, then, with those who charge that a comparison analysis fails, in many cases, to provide an exact paraphrase of metaphors. But I disagree with the additional claim, of Black and Hesse, that the failure occurs because use of the metaphor changes the meaning of (at least) one of the component terms. Such a change of meaning may come about, but often it does not; and even where it does come about, it will not hamper our attempts to paraphrase the metaphor exactly. What will hamper our attempts to find an exact paraphrase is the scarcity of pairs of synonyms, including both single words and phrases, which are exactly equivalent in meaning. This same scarcity will make it difficult to find exact paraphrases in some cases, although perhaps not as many, where metaphor is not involved at all. That we cannot find an exact paraphrase, or translation, of a statement, however, does not entail that such a statement cannot be understood. We probably cannot find an exact paraphrase of a statement such as "John Stuart Mill was very intelligent," for there is no word, or set of words, exactly equivalent in meaning to the word "intelligent." Yet, we would not thereby conclude that this statement is incomprehensible. To explain what is being said, it is not necessary to find an exact paraphrase or translation; giving a rough paraphrase, or explaining in some other way, is sufficient. To explain is not to translate, at least not necessarily.

We need not say, then, that all metaphors are meaningless. In using words metaphorically, a speaker is not making the same statement—a statement that might be meaningless—as he would be making if he were to use these same words literally. He is making some other statement, assuming that he is making a statement at all. This other statement, in turn, is not (or, at least, need not be) meaningless either. In most cases of metaphor, we can explain, to some extent, what statement is being made by pointing

121

to another statement which is *roughly* equivalent and whose meaningfulness is not problematic. We can, for example, explain to some extent what is being said when I say, "Man is a wolf." What I am saying, roughly, but only roughly, is that "Man is like a wolf (in certain respects)." There is not, or at least there should not be, any temptation to regard this latter statement as meaningless.

3

I have spoken of "change in meaning" as if it were an abrupt kind of event. This is misleading. The term "fork," for example, did not change in meaning at 3 A.M., Thursday, April 14, 1867—nor at any other precise time. The case of dead metaphors, in fact, nicely illustrates the *transitional* aspect of changes in meaning. An expression which becomes a dead metaphor passes through a transitional phase often lasting many years, during which it is difficult, if not impossible, to say whether the expression is literal or metaphorical. For example, the expression "fork in the road" was first used as a metaphor around 1839.[17] It was subsequently used by enough speakers of English on enough occasions eventually to become a dead metaphor; that is, "fork" was subsequently used often enough to refer to a "branch or break in the road" for this sense of the term to be listed in the dictionary as a separate, literal sense. There was a period, however, between 1839 and the time the expression became a dead metaphor when it would have been very difficult and perhaps impossible to decide whether "fork in the road" was metaphorical.

There are also expressions which at present seem to be in a similar transitional state. For instance, is it a metaphorical or literal use of "blue" to say: "I am not a bit blue about the prospect of losing my wife?" The *Oxford English Dictionary* lists this sense of "blue" as figurative, whereas *Webster's New International* lists it as literal. However, it is probably neither definitely figurative nor definitely literal. In speaking of a change in meaning, then, we should not think of it as similar to a change in facial expression or a change in a woman's attitude; that is, we should not think of it as occurring abruptly. Insofar as I have spoken of "meaning change" in this way, then, I have been speaking misleadingly. But I think it also

[17] *The Oxford English Dictionary,* s. v. "fork."

misleading to say, as some philosophers have said, that the fact that meaning change is often a matter of slow transition shows that there is no clear distinction between metaphorical and literal use. If this means simply that there are expressions which we logically cannot classify correctly as either "metaphorical" or "literal," then I think it is true. I disagree, however, if what is being asserted is that there is no clear distinction between such expressions as: (1) "In very deed the hills were liars, and the multitude of the mountains" (Jean de St. Thomas), and (2) "John has gone downtown to buy a pair of shoes" (Jerry Fodor). There *is* a clear distinction here: the first is clearly metaphorical; the second is clearly not.

A simple and not very original metaphor may be of some help here. We might think of a distinction as a boundary-line drawn between two states. Or, to make the analogy more exact, think of the boundary not as a geometrical line having no width, but as an area one mile wide, bounded on each side by parallel lines. Some houses are located within the one mile area. Many other houses are located clearly on one or the other side of the border. So, too, there are expressions which are in the border area between the literal and metaphorical and expressions located clearly on one or the other side of the boundary.

One additional point. In referring to the expression "Nature is a machine," I said that how a speaker used this expression might depend, in part, on his *intentions*. I shall now say something about this subject of "the speaker's intentions," without moving very far, however, into what is an intricate and involved subject.

As I have already argued, an author may use the same words literally or metaphorically, and, hence, make either of two statements—the first of which may be meaningless, while the second is not. To determine whether we are confronted with metaphor or nonsense, therefore, we must determine what is being said—what statement is actually being made. To determine this we *may* have to consider the author's intentions. If I say in the abstract, for example, that "the hills were liars," you may have to determine how I intend to use these words, before condemning me for speaking nonsensically, or pardoning me for speaking metaphorically. The same is true where other linguistic devices are employed, such as irony, metonymy, hyperbole, etc. You may, once again, have to ascertain the author's intentions to decide what is being said. *If* this is necessary, but cannot be done—perhaps because the author is dead and the text itself is silent—then we may be unable to determine what is being said, and, therefore, may be unable to determine if what is being said is meaningless.

Ascertaining intentions, however, is not always necessary. It is not necessary, for example, if the speaker clearly indicates how he is to be understood, perhaps by using some contextual device such as raising his voice or marking "poetry" above his words. Brutus, for example, clearly indicated how he was to be understood when he said, in an ironic tone of voice, "Caesar is an honorable man." In using an ironic contour, he indicated that he was not lauding Caesar for being *honorable,* but denigrating him for being *dishonorable.* In such a case, the author's actual, and perhaps hidden, intentions do not alter what is being said. Brutus, for example, might have subsequently denied that he intended to defame Caesar; but, nevertheless, he did. So, too, if a man says in an everyday context, "John went downtown to buy a pair of shoes," we need not consider the speaker's intentions at all, once we know who "John" is. Apart from some extraordinary context, these words could be used to mean but one thing.[18] In general, what a *speaker* means is what he intends to say; but what his *words* mean may not be what *he* means, and, hence, may not mean what he intends to say. We sometimes fail to say what we mean—we intend to say one thing but actually say another. It is what we actually say, however, and not (necessarily) what we intend to say, that is either meaningless or meaningful.

I shall now summarize what I have been saying in this chapter.

1. Some philosophers have charged that metaphors are category mistakes, or at least meaningless for some other reason. I tried to show that this view is mistaken, and in what way. In many cases, a meaningless statement would result if a sentence were being used literally. In the case of a metaphor, however, the sentence is not being used literally, and some statement other than the literal, meaningless statement is being made. There is no need to conclude, therefore, that all metaphors are meaningless. It might be meaningless, for example, to assert literally that "thoughts smell in the rain"; but if a poet, such as Dylan Thomas, uses these words,

[18] For a useful discussion of this subject see: J. A. Fodor, "What Do You Mean?" *Journal of Philosophy,* LVII (1960), pp. 499–506.

then he may be speaking not literally but metaphorically. He may, therefore, be making a different statement from that which would be made if he were speaking literally. His statement, moreover, may be meaningful. In metaphorical usage, then, something other than the literal, meaningless statement is being made. But what is this other statement? Is *it* meaningful? If it is not, then metaphors, once again, will be said to be meaningless. In answering this question, I considered first the comparison view of metaphor, according to which the other statement being made is equivalent to another statement which makes a comparison of some kind. For example, "Man is a lion," when used metaphorically, means "Man is like a lion."

2. Max Black and others, such as Mary Hesse, have recently argued, however, that a supplementary analysis of metaphor is needed. According to this supplementary analysis, the predicate-term "interacts" with the subject-term in certain metaphors so as to cause a change in meaning of the latter (or of both). Saying that "Man is a wolf," for example, changes the meaning of "man"—man seems more wolf-like than before the use of the metaphor. For this reason, no literal paraphrase of the metaphor will do. In giving a literal paraphrase, we are using "man" in its former sense, and "man" does not now have this sense. Black's argument has been quite influential and is cited by a number of recent writers on metaphor. I have argued, however, that the argument is unsound.[19] Using a metaphor, any metaphor whatsoever, *may* cause a change in meaning, but probably it will not. Moreover, if a change in meaning does come about, this will not in itself affect our ability to find a suitable paraphrase. Hence, the interaction analysis does not explain why the comparison analysis fails to fit complex metaphors.

3. There are many cases, it is true, in which no more than a *rough* paraphrase is to be found. For this reason, a comparison view of metaphor is too simplistic: not all metaphors admit of *exact* paraphrase. But neither do all literal statements. The reason, in both instances, has to do not with meaning change, but with the melancholy fact that few synonyms, if any, are *exactly* equivalent in meaning.

[19] I have not objected, however, to any of the other interesting points which Black makes about metaphor, nor have I tried to present a rival account of how metaphors function.

chapter vi

a theory of meaninglessness

In this last chapter, I shall try to construct a theory of meaninglessness, that is, a somewhat systematic account of the correct use of the concept I have been discussing. In giving such a systematic account, one must, I think, deal with the skepticism and hostility a growing number of philosophers feel toward the use of this concept in solving philosophic problems. I have already tried to do so, in part, by discussing the claims and arguments of what I have termed "moderate" and "radical" skepticism.

On the one side, I have challenged the radical skeptic's assertion that it is altogether futile to seek criteria of meaninglessness, not because there are no criteria, but because the concept of meaninglessness is radically and irreparably defective. I have argued, for example, against those who hold that what is meaningless in one language may be meaningful in another, that what is meaningless at one time may be meaningful at a later time, and that use of the concept of meaninglessness compels us to condemn as nonsense certain metaphors that we would ordinarily believe to be meaningful. If I have argued successfully against such claims, then a radical skepticism about the use of the concept of meaninglessness is not justified.

On the other side, however, I have agreed with, and tried to demonstrate, the moderate skeptic's contention that the general, standard criteria of meaninglessness are all inadequate. The following question then arises: if we do not have any adequate general criteria of meaninglessness, should we not, in all good conscience and despite the failure of radical skepticism, cease using the concept? I shall take up the question of criteria first and then proceed to discuss related topics.

1

The first point I wish to make is that we should distinguish, in a way that I have not yet done, between the demand for a general *criterion* of meaninglessness and the demand for a general *test* of meaninglessness. It is true that "test" and "criterion" are sometimes used interchangeably, but these terms cannot be readily exchanged in *all* contexts. If I say that I have a test for distinguishing a good newspaper from a bad newspaper, I might justifiably say that I have a criterion for distinguishing a good newspaper from a bad one. On the other hand, "correspondence to the facts" may be a criterion of "truth," in that a statement is true if it corresponds to the facts, and yet not provide us with a *test* of truth (or, at the very least, with a *useful* test of truth). If we doubted whether a statement were true, we would very probably be in doubt as to whether the statement corresponded to the facts. To use a somewhat obscure metaphor that nevertheless may be helpful—"being in accordance with the facts" is on the same level of abstraction as the term "true."

In the same way, we do have a criterion of "meaningless" in "neither true nor false": a statement is meaningless if it is "neither true nor false." Yet, because this expression is on the same level of abstraction as "meaningless," it will not provide us with a useful test of meaninglessness. In any case in which it is unknown whether a statement is meaningless, it would also probably be unknown whether the statement is neither true nor false. We can say, as a result, that if it is simply demanded that there be something to justify calling a particular statement meaningless, the demand can be satisfied: any statement possessing the property of being neither true nor false is meaningless. In this sense, then, there is a general criterion of meaninglessness; however, if "criterion" is used in the sense of "test," I would agree that we lack a general criterion, for we do not have any general test, at least not any *useful* general test, for deciding whether a statement is meaningless.

Is, then, the concept of meaninglessness a useless concept? I do not think so. There are many useful concepts for which we lack any general test for determining when they apply. Take, for example, the notion of a self-contradiction. We do not have any useful, general test for determining when a statement is self-contradictory, but that does not mean that the concept is not useful. A similar point can be made about related concepts, such as synonymy, analyticity, and necessary truth: we have no useful, general test for determining when they apply. Some philosophers, of course, would think that sufficient reason to eliminate them along with the concept of meaninglessness. I think, however, that there are good arguments against such a view. Moreover, there is no need to appeal to the employment of "semantic" concepts alone. There are other concepts that do not belong to this same family, for which a similar point can be made. For example, take the concept of a "fruitful theory."[1] We have no one, general test for distinguishing a fruitful theory from a sterile one, for there are many different ways in which a theory may be fruitful. That is not, however, a sufficient reason to stop using the concept. The lack of a general test for meaninglessness does not mean that we should do away with it either.[2]

2

So far, I have argued against radical skepticism and in support of moderate skepticism. In addition, I have now argued that the thesis of moderate skepticism (that there is no adequate test of meaninglessness), although correct, does not require us to abandon the concept of meaninglessness. However, I now want to show that we should, in spite of what I have said so far, abandon this concept in favor of one very much like it that can be used to serve the same essential purposes.

Some philosophers think it quite obvious that certain statements are meaningless, while others think it just as obvious that these same state-

---

[1] I have borrowed this illustration from G. Schlesinger, who introduces it to make a similar point. See his essay, "Operationalism" in Edwards (ed.), *Encyclopedia of Philosophy*, vol. V, p. 546.

[2] Of course, it would be crucial if we had no way at all of knowing when a statement is meaningless. But I shall discuss this point in Section 5.

ments are not meaningless, but instead are false. Among the first group of philosophers is the late Arthur Pap, who writes:

But the distinction between the false and the meaningless is already recognized by common sense apart from any preoccupation with logical theory. 'The theory of relativity is blue,' 'the number 5 weighs more than the number 6,' 'his mind eats fish': these and millions more predications would unhesitatingly be dismissed as meaningless, not false, in spite of their *syntactic* correctness, by plain people.[3] (Pap's italics)

So, too, Paul Benacerraf—in referring to identity statements such as "Caesar is a prime number"—argues:

Some will want to argue that identities of type (C) are not senseless or unsemantical, but simply false—on the grounds that the distinction of categories is one that cannot be drawn. I have only the following argument to counter such a view. It will be just as hard to explain how one *knows* that they are false as it would be to explain how one knows that they are senseless.[4]

A writer such as Quine would disagree with Pap and Benacerraf. He would prefer to treat such statements as self-contradictions—"for the forms concerned would remain still quite under control if admitted rather, like self-contradictions, as false (and false by meaning, if one likes)."[5] Moreover, the ground for such a preference seems to be, as Benacerraf claims, that Quine thinks category distinctions cannot be drawn. If that were the only reason for describing statements such as "Caesar is a prime number" as false, then I think that Pap and Benacerraf would be on firmer ground. It is not that I think that type distinctions can be adequately drawn; on the contrary, I have argued, in effect, that this could not be done when I tried to expose the defects of the category mistake argument. Even if we cannot show that certain statements are meaningless by use of a category criterion, we may be able to show it in some other way. I do not think, then, that our inability to prove that such statements are meaningless by use of a category criterion is sufficient reason for describing such statements as "false"

---

[3] Arthur Pap, "Types and Meaninglessness," *Mind*, LXIX (1960), p. 41.
[4] Paul Benacerraf, "What Numbers Could Not Be," *Philosophical Review*, LXXVIII (1965), p. 66.
[5] Quine, *Word and Object*, p. 229.

130

instead of "meaningless." This is not, however, the only reason for calling such statements "false." A second concerns the negations of statements said to be meaningless.

Suppose we negate a statement such as "Caesar is a prime number," or "Virtue is square." Are the resulting statements—"Caesar is *not* a prime number" and "Virtue is *not* square"—meaningless? Or are they true? Some philosophers are convinced—and believe they can prove—that such statements are true. For example, A. N. Prior tries to prove that "Virtue is not square" is true, rather than meaningless, by arguing: "My proof that virtue is not square is a simple syllogism—what is square has some shape, but virtue has no shape, therefore, virtue is not square."[6]

If we accept such a proof, and make the further assumption made by most philosophers that the negation of a true statement must be false, then it would seem that we have to say that a statement such as "Virtue is square" is not meaningless, but false. Thus, if "Virtue is not square" is true rather than meaningless, then "Virtue is square" is also not meaningless, but false. Is such reasoning, then, powerful enough to overthrow the assertions of philosophers such as Pap and Benacerraf? It is likely to be objected here that Prior is begging the question. If we have already accepted that "Virtue is not square" is true rather than meaningless, then, of course, we could also accept the truth of Prior's second premise, that "Virtue has no shape." But the proof would then be worthless, since we would already accept what we are trying to prove. If we do not accept the meaningfulness of the conclusion, then we are not likely to accept the meaningfulness of Prior's second premise either. "Virtue has no shape" surely has the same status as "Virtue is not square": *if* the latter is obviously meaningless, then so is the former.

I would reply to the above objection by contending that neither "Virtue is not square" nor "Virtue has no shape" is obviously meaningless. Suppose, for example, that I wish to explain to a child what kinds of things either are or could be square. I might point out that although clocks, or even clouds, could be square, virtue, not being in space, does not have a shape of any kind. Hence, virtue is not, and could not be, square. I concede

---

[6] A. N. Prior, "Entities," *Australasian Journal of Philosophy*, XXXII (1954), p. 159.

that a child might think he understands my explanation and yet be mistaken. So, too, although I think *I* understand what it is like for virtue not to have a shape and not to be square, I too may be mistaken. My point, however, is that it is not obvious that I am mistaken. It needs to be argued, and not merely asserted, that "Virtue is not square" and "Virtue has no shape" are meaningless.

Some philosophers would argue, I think, that "Virtue is not square" must be meaningless *because* it is a presupposition of being either square or not square that the object have some shape. But surely virtue, unlike a clock or a cloud, has no shape; and, hence, one of the presuppositions of saying that virtue is not square does not hold. Such a statement, then, is meaningless. This argument has two defects. In the first place, the proponent of this argument has no right to assert, "Surely, virtue has no shape." If he assumes that this assertion is true—rather than meaningless—then the kind of proof that Prior constructed could be used to show that "Virtue is not square" is also true. The second defect lies in the assumption that "saying of any X that it is square or not square presupposes that it has some shape or other." This assumption is plausible enough if restricted to the assertion "X is square," for it can be plausibly argued that in order for any X to be square it is logically necessary that it have a shape to begin with. It is not so obvious that this same assumption extends to the negative assertion that "X is *not* square." Why cannot something that has no shape be not square? It would seem, in fact, that it must be the case that anything having no shape is not square. Some philosophers, I think, would wish to object to this assertion on the grounds that if I say that something is not square I imply that it has some shape other than squareness. This objection is merely a restatement of the original assumption about the presuppositions of the statement, unless, of course, we distinguish—as some philosophers do—between presupposition and implication; but, even if we do make such a distinction, this new claim would be just as doubtful as the original assumption. Although it may be true when I say that *some* Xs are not square that I imply, or at least suggest, that they have some shape other than squareness, that does not seem to be true of *all* Xs, although it may be true of clouds and clocks. For example, when I say that a clock is not square, perhaps I do imply that it has some other shape: a clock necessarily has some shape or other. That is not true of such things as virtue, for virtue, unlike a cloud or a clock, does not necessarily have a shape. Far from it. At any rate, some argument must be developed to show that my denying that virtue is square does carry this implication with it. I know of no such argument and conclude, then, that the argument which makes use of the dubious assumption that "my saying of any X that it is not square presupposes that it has some shape to begin with" is unconvincing.

One further argument that is sometimes made is that we must distinguish between the negation of a whole statement and the negation of a predicate. If we make this distinction, we can say that the negation of the meaningless statement "Virtue is square" is true, for the negation of the whole statement would read: "It is not the case that virtue is square." On the other hand, the negation of the predicate, according to this view, would be just as meaningless as the affirmation of the predicate. Thus, "Virtue is not square," which would be the negation of the predicate and not of the whole statement, would be meaningless.

I can see no objection to making a distinction between the negation of a predicate and the negation of a statement. Moreover, making such a distinction would enable us to affirm such statements as "Virtue is not square" by merely prefixing, "It is the case that. . . ." That would be advantageous, however, only if we did not already have the means of making such affirmations, but we can make such an affirmation by saying, simply and truly, that "Virtue is not square." Only if we already assume that such affirmations are meaningless, rather than true, will the need for distinguishing statement-negation from predicate-negation arise. The argument, therefore, does not show that the negations of meaningless statements are not true. It merely assumes it.

There may be some further argument that would show that the negations of so-called meaningless statements are meaningless, but I know of no such argument. Henceforth, then, I shall assume that such statements as "Virtue is not square" are not meaningless. It might be objected here that I still have not shown that "Virtue is not square" is true. Even if Prior's assumption that virtue has no shape is not obviously meaningless, and even if it cannot be proved to be meaningless, nevertheless the truth of the assumption still needs to be demonstrated. In reply, I could argue that virtue is not in space, and anything which is not in space has no shape. Hence, Prior's assumption is true. However, the objector might then ask me to prove that virtue is not in space. At this point, I might try to show that, given what is meant by "virtue," virtue is not the kind of thing that could be in space. In showing that, however, I would still have to rely on certain assumptions, and any assumptions I rely on might, in turn, be challenged. For this reason, a satisfactory demonstration that "Virtue is not square" is true might involve a long series of arguments. Rather than try to run through the entire demonstration, I shall simply assume that such a demonstration could be given. If this seemingly plausible assumption were to prove false, my first reason for abandoning "meaninglessness" in the sense of "neither true nor false" would be inadequate. If this were to happen, I would then rely solely on the two additional reasons which I shall give later.

I shall assume, then, that the negations of allegedly meaningless statements are true rather than meaningless (or false, where the allegedly meaningless statements are true). If we further assume that the negation of a true statement must be false, we must also say that the statements being negated (again excluding those which, in fact, are true), such as "Virtue is square," are also not meaningless, but are false. The only question left, then, is whether we should assume that the negation of a true statement must be false. Here it is relevant to point out that the positivists, and most others who have wanted to use "meaningless" to mean "neither true nor false," have made this assumption. In fact, some of these philosophers have explicitly appealed to either this assumption or its converse (that the negation of a false statement must be true) in trying to prove that certain statements are neither true nor false. For example, R. Routley tries to show that "The number seven dislikes dancing" is neither true nor false by the following argument.[7] The negation of "The number seven dislikes dancing" is "The number seven doesn't dislike dancing." This second statement is not true, but the negation of a false statement must be true. Hence, the initial statement, "The number seven dislikes dancing," is not false: it is neither true nor false.

[7] Routley, "On a Significance Theory," p. 181.

The weakness of Routley's argument, however, is that it assumes—without additional argument—that the statement "The number seven doesn't dislike dancing" is not true. Someone might think this statement to be not true because he believes that it implies the absurdity, "The number seven likes dancing." (It would be unjust, however, to attribute this belief to Routley; he does not say why he accepts the above assumption.) That belief, however, is mistaken. I do not dislike dancing, but it does not follow, and in fact is false, that I like dancing. The truth is: I neither like nor dislike dancing; I have no opinion about the matter. So, too, for the number seven: the number seven does not have an opinion about dancing, or about anything else. Therefore, it does not dislike dancing or anything else. The statement "The number seven doesn't dislike dancing" is therefore true.

Most philosophers, then, who have used "meaningless" to mean "neither true nor false" would accept the assumption that a negation of a true statement must be false; therefore, they would, or should, accept the further conclusion that a statement such as "Virtue is square" is false, once they agree that the negation of such a statement is true. I can see no good reason, moreover, for rejecting the assumption that the negation of a true statement is false. The reason we make such an assumption has, of course, to do with the meaning of the word "not." For example, if the atomic number of iron is 26, then it is true that "The atomic number of iron is not 25." It follows, then, given the meaning of "not," that it is false that "The atomic number of iron is not not 25." But this statement says the same as "The atomic number of iron is 25"; hence, if one is false, then so is the other. So, too, if "Virtue is not square" is true, then it is false that "Virtue is not not square." But this last statement says the same as "Virtue is square"; hence, if "Virtue is not not square" is false, it is false that "Virtue is square."

Since my argument concerning the negations of statements said to be meaningless holds for all such statements, we now have a good reason for abandoning our use of the term "meaningless," insofar as it is interpreted as "neither true nor false." In every case of a putatively meaningless statement, either it, or its negation, is true. For example, the negation of "Saturday is in bed," a statement often said to be meaningless, is "Saturday

135

is not in bed," which is a true statement. If the negation of a true statement is false, then it follows that all putatively meaningless statements (except for those which are true) are false. Hence, there are no meaningless statements in the sense in which "meaningless" means "neither true nor false."

The above reason, moreover, is not the only reason to cease using "meaningless" to mean "neither true nor false." A second reason concerns the kind of thing which is said to be meaningless. Most philosophers who have used this concept have assumed that sentences, and not statements, propositions, and the like, are either meaningful or meaningless. This assumption led many in the first place to interpret "meaningless" as "neither true nor false." If we accept this assumption, then, it seems reasonable to say that such a sentence as "The theory of relativity is blue" is neither true nor false. Philosophers who make this assumption generally contend that such a sentence is meaningless *because* it cannot be used to make a statement; but since only statements can be either true or false, it seems reasonable to declare that such a sentence is not only not true, but is also not false; hence, it is neither true nor false. This line of reasoning, however, should be rejected on a number of counts.

First, if only statements, propositions, and such—and not sentences —are either true or false, no sentence whatsoever is either true or false. Thus, if "meaningless" meant "neither true nor false," even sentences which clearly could be used to make statements would also be meaningless, for they, too, would be neither true nor false. Second, it is false that a sentence such as "The theory of relativity is blue" cannot be used to make a statement; it can even be used to make a true statement. Third, there is no logical bar preventing our speaking coherently of statements as meaningless. Finally, most philosophers who have *used* the concept of meaninglessness have, in fact, spoken this way, despite what they might have said when talking *about* "meaninglessness." They did not condemn a particular sentence as meaningless, but only a particular statement which might be made by using the sentence. For example, although Ayer condemned as meaningless the statement customarily made by the use of the sentence "Stealing money is wrong," he did not censure the sentence itself. Ayer would readily admit that the sentence was innocent of any logical defect when, for example, the term "wrong" was used to mean "disapproved of by most members of my society." It is a mistake, therefore, to think that "meaningless" must mean "neither true nor false" *because* sentences and only sentences can be meaningless, for it is false that only sentences can be meaningless. (For the arguments for these claims, see chapter IV.)

A third reason for abandoning the concept "meaningless" in the sense in which it means "neither true nor false" is that there is another concept closely resembling it which can be used for most, if not all, of the significant philosophic purposes for which the original concept has been used, and whose use does not involve us in the same difficulties as the original. The concept I have in mind is the concept of "meaninglessness" as it is used to mean "a priori false."[8]

Philosophers originally began using the concept of meaninglessness mainly because they thought it was useful in resolving certain philosophic disputes. For example, Ayer thought he could resolve the traditional dispute between the theist and atheist by demonstrating that the statement "God exists" is meaningless; and Ryle contended that disputes about the mind-body relation could be settled by showing that the statement "Minds and bodies exist" is meaningless (or, as he preferred to phrase it, "absurd"). These disputes could just as easily have been settled by showing that the statements in question are a priori false, rather than neither true nor false. It is thought to be important that we can know a priori that such statements are not true because the available empirical evidence often does not definitely favor or disfavor the statement in question; but it is not important, for philosophical purposes, to know a priori that such statements are neither true nor false.

It is not clear that when we interpret "meaningless" to mean "a priori false" we are departing from the way nonphilosophers use the term—despite what Arthur Pap says. It is not clear that when, as Pap claims, "plain

---

[8] I assume that this interpretation of "meaningless" is consonant with Quine's suggestion that allegedly meaningless statements should be said to be false "and false by meaning if one likes." I am also influenced here, and elsewhere, by the very sensible suggestions of Arthur Pap and Theodore Drange. I reject, however, their interpretations of "meaningless" as, respectively, "synthetic a priori false" and "neither true nor empirically false." The first interpretation contains, unnecessarily, a very controversial component (that of the synthetic a priori); the second leaves open the question whether meaningless statements are false, and, for reasons already given, I do not think this question should be left open. See Quine, *Word and Object*, p. 229; Pap, "Types and Meaninglessness," p. 53; and Drange, *Type Crossings*, p. 23.

people" describe such statements as "The theory of relativity is blue" as meaningless, they mean that such a statement is not only not true but is not false either. What *is* being said, I think, is that such statements are not only not true, but also that they are unintelligible, in that we cannot understand what it would be like for them to be true. It is not so clear, however, that it is also being claimed that such statements are not false either. At any rate, such a claim would be otiose, for as Pap himself points out, the important distinction is between statements such as "The theory of relativity was proposed by Isaac Newton" and "The theory of relativity is blue"—that is, between statements that happen to be false, but might have been true, and statements whose truth is not intelligible to us. There seems no good reason, however, to make the additional assertion that some statements, i.e., the meaningless statements, are not only not empirically false, but are not false at all. I have, moreover, already given reason for thinking that such statements, in fact, are false.

Finally, using "meaningless" to mean "a priori false" would spare us some of the difficulties associated with "neither true nor false." Now we can agree that a statement such as "Virtue is not square" is true and agree, nevertheless, that its negation is meaningless, without giving up the well-entrenched assumption that the negation of a true statement is false. We can now say that its negation, "Virtue is square," is both meaningless and false; it is a priori false.[9] I conclude, then, that we should abandon the concept of "meaninglessness" in the sense in which this term means "neither true nor false," and that we should replace it with the notion "a priori false." Henceforth, then, I will interpret "meaningless" as meaning "a priori false."

3

Using "meaningless" to mean "a priori false" generates a new problem. Are not self-contradictory statements, such as "Some bachelors are

---

[9] Some philosophers speak of a priori *statements,* while others speak only of the *knowledge* that such statements are true (or false) as being a priori. I prefer to follow the lead of the former group and speak of certain statements as being a priori false, so as to leave open the question whether these same statements are either analytic or synthetic.

married," also a priori false? I agree that the answer to this question is affirmative, but, then, such statements would be meaningless. Philosophers have often resisted the temptation to describe contradictions as meaningless, for they wanted to say that such statements are false. If, however, "meaningless" means "a priori false," and not "neither true nor false," then this reason evaporates, for contradictions can now be described as both meaningless and false. Moreover, it is quite appropriate to link such statements as "Some bachelors are married" and "Virtue is square"; both kinds of statements are unintelligible in that we cannot understand what it would be like for them to be true. I conclude, then, that it is not objectionable that contradictions turn out to be meaningless, if we interpret "meaningless" as meaning "a priori false."

For certain purposes, we may still wish to distinguish contradictions from other kinds of meaningless statements. I know of no very precise way of doing this; however, the following may provide a rough means of making the required distinction. We might begin by dividing a priori truths into those true by virtue of their logical form, those reducible by substitution of synonyms to statements of the first kind, and those falling into neither of the first two kinds. For example, "A bachelor is a bachelor" is a statement of the first kind; and "A bachelor is an unmarried male" is a statement of the second kind. The second statement is not true by virtue of its logical form, but it can be reduced to such a statement by replacing "unmarried male" with the synonym "bachelor," leaving the result, "A bachelor is a bachelor." The result, once again, is a statement true by virtue of its logical form. There are also a priori truths that do not fall into either of the first two groups. Examples are: "Virtue is not square" and "The theory of relativity is not blue."

To draw the distinction we want, the expression "contradiction" should be restricted to the negation of statements of the first two kinds. Thus, "A bachelor is not a bachelor" and "A bachelor is not an unmarried male" would be contradictions, but "Virtue is square" and "The theory of relativity is blue" would not. The latter two would be meaningless but not self-contradictory. The use of "contradiction" that I am advocating is, of course, not new. Many philosophers and logicians, though not all, have restricted the application of this expression to denials of the first two kinds of a priori truths, and there is some rationale for restricting the use of the expression in this way. The first two kinds of denials either have the logical form of "P and not P," or are reducible without change of meaning to statements having this form. This is not true, though, of the third kind of statement, such as "Virtue is not square." Nevertheless, I am not insisting that it is definitely wrong to describe this third kind of statement as self-contradictory. I am merely pointing out that by restricting the scope of "contradiction" to the first two kinds of statements, as many philosophers do anyway, we can distinguish, in a rough way, between contradictions and other kinds of meaningless statements. Some statements, however, will be difficult to classify even if we do draw this distinction. Further, in many contexts there would be no good reason even to attempt such a classification. In many contexts, what we are interested in may be simply whether a given statement is a priori false—not whether it belongs to a particular species of a priori falsehood. Finally, in attempting to draw the above distinction, I have used concepts such as "synonymy" and "logical form." I do not mean to suggest, in doing so, that such notions are totally free from the taint of obscurity. That would be false. I do think that these concepts are clear enough to be used in drawing some distinction, although a rough one, between contradictions and noncontradictory, meaningless statements.

If we do decide to make such a distinction, should we describe the noncontradictory statements as "synthetic," as Arthur Pap has suggested? Should we then say, for example, that "Virtue is square" is a synthetic a priori falsehood? I do not know how to answer this question in any simple, straightforward way, but the following comments may help.

To begin with, some philosophers define "synthetic a priori" in such a way that the concept fits only true statements. If we do the same, of course, there can be no synthetic a priori falsehoods. On the other hand, some philosophers define "synthetic a priori" in such a way that a priori statements which are not self-contradictory and whose negations are not self-contradictory are synthetic. If we use "synthetic" in this way, then the question "Are there synthetic a priori falsehoods?" turns, in large part, on how we use the notion of a contradiction. If we restrict "contradiction" to the first two kinds of a priori false statements that I spoke of earlier, then there would be synthetic a priori falsehoods. For example, "Virtue is square" would be a priori false, but not self-contradictory; hence, it would be a synthetic a priori falsehood. If we do not restrict "contradiction" in the manner I have suggested, but include all a priori falsehoods as contradictions, we would be left without any synthetic a priori falsehoods. All meaningless statements, then, would be contradictions. My first point, then, is that given the array of definitions of "synthetic a priori," you must choose one such definition before you can answer the question, "Are there synthetic a priori falsehoods?" Moreover, given that "synthetic a priori" is a technical term, and given that it has been used by philosophers in a variety of ways, I do not think that there is one and only one correct interpretation of the term.

Some philosophers would regard these comments as purely verbal and as having no bearing on the most important question concerning allegedly synthetic a priori statements. What we really want to know, these philosophers might say, is whether there are any a priori statements that are informative. There is some historical justification for framing the question in this way, for Kant and other philosophers have sometimes contrasted synthetic a priori statements with nonsynthetic (analytic) a priori statements, which were said to be trivial and noninformative. If the question is framed in this way, I think we have the right to ask a further question: to whom are such statements said to be informative? What is informative depends not merely on the statement being made, but also on the listener and on his background of information. For example, consider the a priori statement, "A man ought to do what he ought to do." In all of the standard interpretations of "synthetic," this statement would not be synthetic: it would be an example of an analytic a priori statement. Yet, this statement could very well be informative to some people. It could be informative if it is true, as some philosophers contend, that men are sometimes mistaken in thinking they ought to do something. We might use it, for example, to impart information to someone who concedes that men are sometimes mistaken as to what their duty is (men sometimes believe, for example, that they should wage a particular war when, in fact, they should not, etc.) and yet believes, unthinkingly, that a man should *always* do what he thinks is right (that is, that sometimes a man ought to do what he ought not to do). So, even a rather trivial analytic a priori statement could be informative.

Moreover, it is not likely that all a priori statements are so trivial. For example, a statement such as "Thoughts are not in space" has often been alleged to be an a priori truth. Should it, or any other such controversial example, turn out to be an a priori truth, however, then at least one a priori statement would prove to be informative. For example, if I mistakenly believe that thoughts are in space, then I am given information when I am told that thoughts are not in space. I conclude, then, that it is probable that at least some a priori statements are informative; i.e., they could be used in certain contexts to impart information. This in itself does not imply that it is probable that there are synthetic a priori statements, for it might turn out that all informative a priori statements are analytic. Moreover, even if we do speak of synthetic a priori falsehoods, we should not speak of this type of synthetic a priori statement as informative. I do not give you information when I tell you, for example, that virtue is square; at best, I mislead you. To give information is to communicate knowledge, and to tell you something false is not to give you knowledge.

A final point should be made. The claim that there are synthetic a priori statements has often been identified with the claim that there are statements which can be known to be true (or false) by means of rational insight. This latter claim is particularly controversial and is hard to evaluate without prior clarification of the phrase "rational insight." For this reason I believe it would be unwise to define "meaningless" as "synthetic a priori false." Instead, we should be content to speak of meaningless statements as being a priori false. We can then try to answer the question: are any meaningless statements synthetic (or, are there any synthetic a priori falsehoods)? My answer here, to sum up this discussion, is that it depends in part on the question being asked. On some interpretations of "synthetic" and on some interpretations of "contradiction" there are no synthetic a priori falsehoods; but on other interpretations of these two notions, there are such statements.

I should now retrace some of what I have been saying. After arguing that neither "radical" nor "moderate" skepticism, in the sense I have defined these terms, provides sufficient reason for repudiating "meaningless" in the sense of "neither true nor false," I gave my own reasons for such a rejection. These reasons concerned the negations of statements said to be meaningless; the fact that "meaningless," if it is to be used at all, should be predicated of statements, not sentences; and the fact that there is a similar concept which serves the same essential purposes and serves them better. This similar concept is that of a priori falsity. I then pointed out that if we interpret "meaningless" as "a priori false," contradictions will turn out to be meaningless. I tried to explain, however, why this is not objectionable.

We can, if we wish, draw a distinction between contradictions and other kinds of meaningless statements. If we do draw such a distinction, then we can say that noncontradictory, meaningless statements are synthetic a priori falsehoods on some interpretations of "synthetic a priori," but not on others. In any event, we should not try, for the reasons given, to build the notion of the synthetic a priori into the very definition of "meaningless."

4

I should now like to consider what some philosophers would take to be a decisive objection to the view I have been presenting. One of my main reasons for rejecting "meaningless" in the sense of "neither true nor false" is that there are no meaningless statements in this sense. It will be objected by some, however, that there is at least one class of statements that are neither true nor false. These statements are sometimes described as "reference-failures." To answer this objection, then, I need to examine in detail the theory of reference on which it is based.

According to this theory, certain statements containing subject-expressions that fail to refer to any existing thing are neither true nor false. For example, the subject expression "the king of France" does not refer to any existing thing in the statement which would be made today if we asserted that "the king of France is wise," for today France does not have a king. The statement, then, is neither true nor false.

The chief proponent of this widely accepted view of reference is P. F. Strawson. Strawson does not conceive his account of reference, however, as providing a way of proving that certain statements are meaningless. In fact, he believes that one of the reasons that a certain false view of referring was once accepted is that the trichotomy "either true, false, or meaningless" has been applied to statements.[10] But this trichotomy, he claims, contains a confusion between sentences and statements. Sentences, but not statements, are either meaningful or meaningless; and statements, but not sentences, are either true or false. For example, the sentence "The king of France is wise" is meaningful—that is, it can be used to make a statement—but it is neither true nor false. The statement we would be making if we now used these words to make a statement, and if there now existed a king of France, would be either true or false; it would not be either meaningful or meaningless. But, and this is a crucial element of Strawson's account, if there is no king of France, then the statement we would now be making by uttering the words "The king of France is wise" would be neither true nor false.

I disagree with Strawson's claim that the trichotomy "true, false, or meaningless" is illegitimate. In opposition, I would argue that there need be no conceptual mistake, or confusion of any kind, in speaking of statements as true, false, or meaningless, and that saying that a sentence is meaningful (in the sense that it can be used to make a statement) is to say something of little or no philosophic interest. Since I have already argued for both of these contentions, it would be gratuitous to present the relevant arguments here.[11] Instead, I would merely point out that if Strawson's own account of reference is correct, then he himself has shown that some statements are "meaningless" (in at least one sense of the term), for as used by the positivists and others, "meaningless" means "neither true nor false." Thus, if certain statements are neither true nor false, as Strawson contends, then they are, by definition, meaningless in the positivists' sense of the term. Moreover, it would follow that I am wrong in saying that there are no statements which are "meaningless" in the sense of being "neither true nor false."

One might reply to this by saying that there is something wrong with this use of the term "meaningless," for if the statement "The king of France is wise" has to be adjudged meaningless merely because it is neither true nor false, then there is something illegitimate about this use of the term

---

[10] P. F. Strawson, *Introduction to Logical Theory* (New York: John Wiley & Sons, Inc., 1952), see pp. 174 and 184.

[11] The arguments can be found in chapter IV.

"meaningless." Something is meaningless only if it is unintelligible, and the statement "The king of France is wise" is surely not unintelligible.

I would not, however, like to avail myself of this kind of defense. Someone who wished to defend the use of "meaningless," in the sense of "neither true nor false," might object, and rightly so, to this charge of "illegitimacy." Perhaps in the ordinary way, or at least in one of the ordinary ways, of using the term "meaningless," to say that something is meaningless is to say or imply that it is unintelligible. Moreover, it may be that the statement "The king of France is wise" is not unintelligible and yet is neither true nor false. At most, however, this would show that the positivists' use of "meaningless" to mean "neither true nor false" is a technical use. It would not show that the technical use is either illegitimate or unfruitful. Instead of relying on this "illegitimacy" defense, therefore, I want to examine Strawson's view of referring to see if we really must accept the conclusion that reference-failures are statements which are neither true nor false.

Although Strawson's arguments about referring have persuaded many philosophers, I am doubtful about two central elements of his account. These two elements may be presented as follows:

1. A statement such as "The king of France is wise" presupposes that a king of France exists.
2. If the existence presupposition is not met (as when there is no king of France), then a statement such as "The king of France is wise" is neither true nor false.[12]

I shall now present objections to both of the above theses.

Consider that in talking about a fictional character, it is usually clear that we believe that the character being discussed does not exist and may never have existed. For example, in talking about Little Father Time, the boy who commits suicide in Thomas Hardy's novel *Jude the Obscure,* we might assert: "The son of Jude, who is called Little Father Time, is one of

---

[12] See Strawson's essay "On Referring," in *Essays in Conceptual Analysis,* ed. Anthony Flew (New York: St. Martin's Press, 1956), pp. 33–34. In this essay, Strawson speaks of a special sense of "implication," which in his later writings he calls "presupposition."

the strangest fictional characters in all of English literature." In such a statement, the use of the phrase "fictional character" indicates that the speaker does not believe that the person being referred to either exists or ever existed. In such a case, it seems clear that neither the speaker nor the statement he makes presupposes the existence of the person being referred to. Moreover, the same seems to be true in discussing fictional characters when we do not explicitly make use of any such phrase as "fictional character." Thus, when I talk about Hamlet, and say, for example, that Hamlet hated his mother, it seems clear that I do not presuppose that Hamlet exists. There is a difference, it is true, between the statements "The king of France is wise" and "Hamlet hated his mother." The subject expression in the first statement is a definite description (a phrase of the form "The such and such"), while the subject expression in the second statement is a proper name. It is not clear, however, why that should make any difference concerning my point that, in talking about fictional characters, we do not presuppose that they exist. Moreover, it would be simple enough to tell a story about a character who is crowned the king of France. We could then talk about this character and use the very same sentence Strawson uses. That is, in referring to this character, we might state: "The king of France is wise." Since we do not presuppose the existence of fictional characters, there seems no reason to say that statements about them are neither true nor false. There seems to be no reason to say, for example, that the statement "The son of Jude, Little Father Time, is one of the strangest fictional characters in all of English literature" is neither true nor false. In talking about fictional characters, then, it appears to be false both that we presuppose the existence of the character being referred to and that our statements are neither true nor false.

Strawson would probably not disagree with any of the above comments. He does allow that we can speak about fictional characters without presupposing that they exist.[13] He indicates at one point, however, that in doing so we "pretend to refer."[14] He is saying here, if I understand him, that in talking about Hamlet, for example, we are not referring to Hamlet, but instead we are only pretending to refer to him. However, this claim is open to an obvious objection. To talk about someone is, by definition, to

[13] *Ibid.*, p. 35.
[14] *Ibid.*, p. 40. In a footnote, Strawson concedes that this claim is objectionable.

146

refer to him. It is self-contradictory, then, to say that we are not referring to Hamlet, but are only pretending to refer to Hamlet, when we talk about him. Apart from the inconsistency, moreover, it seems clear that in any ordinary sense of "pretending," I was not pretending to refer to Hamlet when I said that Hamlet hated his mother; I was, in fact, referring to Hamlet.

Strawson also says, however, that using an expression to refer to a fictional character is a *secondary* use.[15] This is a more promising reply. It would now be possible for Strawson to say that only when we use referring expressions in a nonsecondary way can we presuppose the existence of the subject being referred to. Strawson would then need to explain why the use of an expression to refer to a fictional character is a secondary use and why in secondary uses, but not in nonsecondary uses, we can talk about subjects without presupposing their existence. Suppose, for example, that "The king of France is a *homosapien*" is a clear-cut counterinstance to Strawson's two theses. (It is not, but let us assume that it is.) It would not do for Strawson to dismiss this counterinstance merely by saying that it is an example of a *biological* use of a referring expression. He would also need to explain the relevant difference between such a statement as "The king of France is wise" and "The king of France is a *homosapien*." So, too, it is not enough to describe a reference to a fictional character as a secondary use of a referring expression. Strawson also needs to explain why we can talk about a fictional character without presupposing that the character exists, but cannot talk about the present king of France without presupposing that he exists. Strawson, however, does not provide such an explanation.

Further, it is not only in talk about fictional characters that we can refer to someone without presupposing that he exists. Suppose, for example, that I am present at the beheading of King Louis XVI. As soon as the king is killed, I might announce to those who are present: "The king of France is dead." Here I need not be presupposing that the person I am referring to, Louis XVI, exists, for I am asserting that he has died, and to die is to cease to exist. Of course, some people believe in existence after death. But not all people accept this belief; and those who do not will probably not presuppose that a man exists when they say he has died. It is

---

[15] Strawson, "On Referring," pp. 35 and 40.

implausible, for example, to assert that all historians who write about Louis XVI presuppose that he still exists. Moreover, in the case where I am present at the death of Louis, my statement that he has died would not have failed to be either true or false; rather, it would have been true. So, too, suppose that someone asserted the following day: "The king of France is still alive." If the speaker were referring to Louis XVI, he would have been making a false statement, not a statement which is neither true nor false. Moreover, even if the speaker did believe that the king of France (i.e., Louis XVI) existed, his use of the expression "the king of France" to refer to Louis XVI would not *in itself* signal an existence presupposition, any more than my similar use of the same expression signalled an existence presupposition when I said that the king of France was dead. Finally, this second speaker might go on to say that Louis XVI, whom he mistakenly believed to be alive, is in the Temple, but would eventually escape from his enemies. "For," this second speaker might continue, "the king of France is wise." This second speaker's last two assertions, "The king of France is in the Temple" and "The king of France is wise," would have the same truth value as his initial statement, "The king of France is alive"; all three statements would be false.

Apart from the above examples, it seems clear that we can and do talk about nonexisting things without either asserting or presupposing (in Strawson's sense of "presupposing") that they exist. We do talk about quarks, the planet Vulcan, the ether, and the abominable snowman, to cite a few examples, without presupposing that such things exist. Moreover, we do make both false statements and true statements about such things. For example, it is true that the ether was never observed, and it is probably false that the abominable snowman exists. So, too, the planet Vulcan was said by Leverrier, and others, to exist between the sun and Mercury. But Leverrier was wrong; there is no such planet. Contemporary physicists talk about quarks. What they say may be true, but the evidence for the existence of quarks is still inconclusive.

If the above examples are really clear instances of talk about nonexistent things (or about things whose existence is at least uncertain), why should philosophers believe that things must exist if you are to make true or false statements about them? There are at least three such reasons.

First, there is Bertrand Russell's belief that the meaning of a referring expression is some object in the world which the expression refers to. Thus, if no such object exists, then the referring expression has no meaning. Since this view has been criticized elsewhere, I will not comment on it here—except to say that Strawson, too, rejects it.[16]

Second, it seems to be true that if there is no one you are talking about, then you are not talking about anyone. It is easy, then, to slide from this seemingly trivial claim to the claim that if you are not talking about anyone who exists, then you are not talking about anyone. But this move, I think, is mistaken. Sometimes the expression "There is an X" is used to mean, or to imply, "X exists." Thus, if I say, "There is no king of France," it seems reasonable to interpret my statement as saying or implying that "No king of France exists." Such an interpretation, however, is not always reasonable. For example, suppose I say that there is an imaginary land called "Utopia," which is described by Thomas More. It would be unreasonable to interpret my statement as either saying or implying that an imaginary land called "Utopia," which is described by Thomas More, exists. In describing Utopia as an imaginary land, I am clearly implying that it does not exist. Of course, one might go on to say that this imaginary land exists in the writings of Thomas More; but, then, the statement would not be incompatible with the statement that this imaginary land does not exist. So, I can say without contradiction that there is an imaginary land which is described by Thomas More, and that the imaginary land described by Thomas More does not exist. To say "there is an imaginary X" is not to say or imply that "an imaginary X exists." The same point can be made about mythical persons and animals. To say, for example, that there is a mythical horse named Pegasus, which is often talked about by philosophers, is not to say or imply that a mythical horse named Pegasus, which is often talked about by philosophers, exists.[17] So, too, if I say that there is at

---

[16] *Ibid.,* p. 31.

[17] Quine has an imaginary philosopher, Mc X, say the following about Pegasus: "If Pegasus *were* not," Mc X argues, "we should not be talking about anything when we use the word; therefore it would be nonsense to say even that Pegasus is not." But Mc X's first premise is false. If Pegasus were not, we should not be talking about anything *which exists,* when we use the word "Pegasus." We would still be talking about something, something that does not exist when we say, for example, that Pegasus does not exist; when we make such a statement we are talking about Pegasus, a mythical creature. See W. O. Quine, "On What There is," *Review of Metaphysics,* II (1948), p. 22.

least one president who is mourned by most Americans, I am not saying that at least one president who is mourned by most Americans exists, for the president I am talking about is dead—he does not exist.

On the other hand, it would not matter if we did interpret "there is an X" as always meaning (or implying) that "X exists." If we do so interpret "there is an X," we should reject what looked like a trivial claim: namely, that if there is no one you are talking about, then you are not talking about someone. Surely you are talking about someone when you talk about King Louis XVI; and you can talk about King Louis XVI now even though he does not exist. So, if we prefer to say, as some philosophers do, that "there is an X" always means or implies that "X exists," then we should not try to defend the claim that if you are not talking about an X which exists, you are not talking about an X. For plainly we can and do talk about Xs, such as King Louis XVI, the ether, and Santa Claus, which do not exist.

In addition to the two reasons considered so far, there is a third reason, one which Strawson presents, for believing that things must exist if you are to make true or false statements about them. Strawson contends that if there is no king of France then the question whether the statement "The king of France is wise" is true or false simply does not arise.[18] In saying this, he is not, I take it, making an empirical claim to the effect that most competent speakers of English would not ask if such a statement were true or false under the described conditions. He offers no empirical evidence to support such a claim; moreover, it is not clear that the truth of such a claim would establish that the statement "The king of France is wise" is neither true nor false. Rather, I think Strawson is saying that it would be a mistake to ask if such a statement were true or false because, presumably, the statement is not true and is not false either. Thus, to say that asking such a question would be a mistake is to assume, and not to prove, that the above statement is neither true nor false. Hence, what Strawson says concerning this example does not provide an independent reason for saying that things must exist if we are to make true or false statements about them.

Still, there seems to be some substance to what Strawson says here, for

[18] Strawson, "On Referring," p. 34.

it does seem odd in the case he describes to say either that a true statement has been made, or that a false statement has been made. I would now like to explain this apparent oddness and, in doing so, to present my own view of the matter.

I do not agree, for reasons given earlier, that "The king of France is wise" is neither true nor false merely because no king of France exists. We can, as I indicated earlier, speak truly (or falsely) about a king of France who no longer exists, or even about a king of France who never existed (but is merely a fictional character). But I do agree that it would be odd to say, in the case Strawson describes, that either a true statement or a false statement had been made. It would be odd, and in fact false, because no statement has been made. We can make a statement about a king of France who does not exist, as well as about one who does exist; in either case, we at least have to talk about a king of France, either an existing one or a nonexisting one. In Strawson's example, this has not been done. We have not talked about a king of France, or anything else, and therefore we have not made a statement about a king of France, or about anything else. So, too, the same result might occur if I say, "The president of the United States is seven feet tall." There does exist a president (and only one president) of the United States: Richard Nixon. Suppose, however, I said that I was not referring to Richard Nixon, nor to anyone (or anything) else. I would not be talking then about anyone (or anything) and hence would not be making a statement about anyone (or anything). So, too, if I say, "All my children are asleep," I may be making a statement, a false statement, even if I have no children; I may do this, for example, if, unknown to me, my children have just been destroyed in an air raid. If I am not talking about my children, or about anything else, when I utter these words, then I am not making a statement at all. In such cases, I am not making a true or false statement simply because I am not making a statement. These cases are very much like those in which a sentence has been written on a blackboard, or has been uttered to practice one's diction, but has not been used to make a statement. Suppose we find written on a blackboard the sentence "He is six feet tall." Is the sentence true, or is it false? The answer is that it is neither. The statement which would be made if this sentence were used to make a statement about someone would be either true or false, but to make such a statement we would have to talk about someone. So, too, we have to talk about someone (or something) if we are to use either the words "The king of France is wise," or "All my children are asleep," to make a statement. In the situations Strawson describes, this has not been done.

If my view is correct, then we do not have to allow what Strawson calls "truth-value gaps," at least not because of cases of reference-failure. We do not have to say that such cases provide counterinstances to the law of the excluded middle, for in such cases, no statement is being made—hence, it is not true that a statement is being made which is neither true nor false. Most logicians, I think, would welcome this result, but the result is an unhappy one for someone who wishes to speak of statements as "meaningless" in the sense of being "neither true nor false." I began by pointing out that if Strawson were correct, contrary to what I have argued, at least some statements would be meaningless in that sense. I have concluded, however, that Strawson is not correct and, further, that reference-failures are not statements which are neither true nor false. Furthermore, even if my account of reference-failures is incorrect and these are statements which are neither true nor false, such cases would still not provide much solace for those who wish to speak of statements as being "meaningless" in the sense of "being neither true nor false." Reference-failures are not instances of the kind of statements which appear in philosophic disputes, except philosophic disputes about reference. Philosophers do not argue about the meaningfulness of "The king of France is wise" in the same way that they argue about "Pain is identical with the stimulation of c-fibers"; they are not interested in the question whether the former is true, but they are concerned that the latter may be true. It would not very much help the defender of "meaningless" as "neither true nor false," then, even if it did turn out that references-failures are genuine statements and yet are neither true nor false.

5

I would now like to turn to the question of how one proves that a statement is "meaningless" in the sense I am using the term, i.e., in the sense of "a priori false." I have four main points I wish to make here.

1. The first point concerns the demand for a general criterion of "meaninglessness." Earlier, I argued that the lack of an adequate general criterion of "meaningless" in the sense of "neither true nor false" need not deter us from using this concept. I would now make the same point concerning "meaningless" in the sense of "a priori false." If it is asked that there be a "criterion" of meaninglessness, in the sense that there be something which makes it true that a particular statement is meaninglessness, then this request can be met. The property of being a priori false makes the possessor of that property meaningless. In this sense, there is a general criterion of meaninglessness. There is, however, no adequate general *test* for determining when a statement is meaningless (i.e., a priori false). Again, this lack need not deter us from using the concept of meaninglessness. There are many other concepts for which we lack an adequate general test of when they apply, and, yet, they are nonetheless useful. The notion of a fruitful theory is one such concept; the concept of a cause is probably another.

2. It is probable that there are meaningless statements—in fact, a large number of them—for which we do not need a test of any kind. These statements, I think, can be known to be meaningless (a priori false) without our proving them to be so, for they are *obviously* meaningless. I have in mind such statements as "The theory of relativity is blue" and "Virtue is square." No philosopher, I take it, would want to say that such statements are true;[19] I have already given reasons for saying that such statements are false rather than neither true nor false. One might want to claim that such statements should be considered empirically false unless it can be proved that they are meaningless, i.e., a priori false. To this objection, I would make two replies.

First, if such statements are not a priori false, but are merely empirically false, there might exist conditions under which they would be true rather than false. It is reasonable then to think that we could describe such conditions. For example, if "The theory of relativity is blue" is really empirical as is "The theory of relativity was proposed by Isaac Newton,"

---

[19] I agree, however, that some other statements might be made by using these same words and that these other statements might be true. For example, if it is old-fashioned to be virtuous and if that is what one is saying when using the words "Virtue is square," then I agree that this statement is true.

then just as we could describe conditions—which might have held—which would make the latter true, we should also be able to describe conditions under which the former would be true. So, too, if "Virtue is square" is really empirical, then we should be able to describe what it would be like for this statement to be true. The inability to give such descriptions, of course, does not conclusively prove that such statements are not empirical, for we might be handicapped by lack of knowledge or by lack of a sufficiently rich imagination. Nevertheless, if no one is able to give such descriptions, then this is some ground—even if not conclusive ground—for believing that the statements in question are a priori false and not merely empirically false.

Second, if there is a problem of how we know that "Virtue is square" is a priori false, then there is also a problem of how we know that it is empirically false. Presumably we do know that such a statement is false. We could, of course, produce some argument to show that it is false, as Prior did. For example, we might point out that only things in space can be square and that virtue is not in space. But this only postpones the problem: how do we know that it is false to say that virtue is in space? Of course, someone might wish to concede that "Virtue is in space" is a priori false, while denying that the same is true of "Virtue is square." But that would concede the main point at issue, for what is at issue is not whether any particular statement can be known without evidence to be a priori false, but whether any statement at all can. Unless we can show that "Virtue is square" is empirically false, without relying on any premises known without evidence to be a priori false, then refusing to admit that such a statement is a priori false *merely because no proof has been given* will be indefensible if we really do know, as I think we do, that "Virtue is not square" is not true. We come to know that such statements are not true, I believe, not by looking at empirical evidence, but rather by reflecting on the meaning, or the use, of the component terms of the statement. This is a controversial topic, however, and much too large a topic to be explored here. I would simply conclude, then, by saying that these two points—that we cannot describe what it would be like for virtue to be square and that it is difficult to explain how we know that "Virtue is square" is false if the statement is merely empirically false—constitute *some* grounds for believing that the statement is meaningless, i.e., a priori false.

3. Even though we have no adequate test of meaninglessness which would be generally applicable, we might be able to develop tests that would be useful in at least some cases. I now want to discuss briefly three such tests. Earlier, in chapter III, I suggested these same three tests as tests of ambiguity; but because of the relation between ambiguity and meaninglessness, these same tests can be used, in some contexts, as criteria of meaninglessness. I should now like to explain how this can be done.

In general, if it can be shown that a term must be ambiguous when intelligibly predicated of two subjects, or two kinds of subjects, then it can be shown that certain statements containing this term are meaningless (i.e., a priori false). For example, if Ryle could have shown, by use of the category mistake argument, that "exist" must be ambiguous if it is to be meaningfully predicated of "mind" and of "body," then he could have shown that it is meaningless to assert that minds and bodies exist. If we do assert that "Minds and bodies exist"—and do not merely use these words in place of two other statements, namely, that "Minds exist" and that "Bodies exist"—then we must be using "exist" either in the sense in which it meaningfully applies to bodies and not to minds, or in the sense in which it meaningfully applies to minds and not to bodies. There is no third alternative. In either case, the statement will be meaningless. If Ryle were right, it would be a priori false that minds "exist" in the sense in which bodies "exist"; conversely, it would be a priori false that bodies "exist" in the same sense that minds do. If Ryle could have proved his case about the ambiguity of "exist," therefore, he could also have proved his case about the meaninglessness of the statement "Minds and bodies exist." He did not prove his case, I argued, for the argument he used is unsound. The general point nevertheless remains: if we can prove ambiguity by means of some other argument, or by using some other criterion than a category criterion, we can also show that certain statements are meaningless. We do have at our disposal other criteria of ambiguity; therefore, we do have a means of proving that certain statements are meaningless.

Take, for example, the statement "Questions and chairs are hard." Quine thinks that this statement is meaningful because he thinks that "hard" is univocal.[20] But I have already argued, in chapter III, that we can

---

[20] Quine, *Word and Object,* p. 130.

refute this claim (about the univocality of "hard") by using the first two ambiguity criteria I cited. To use the first criterion, we have to show that the "positive" implications of using "hard" are different when "hard" is applied to "questions" from what they are when "hard" is applied to "chairs." Saying that a question is hard implies that it is difficult, but saying that a chair is hard does not. Of course, I may be able to give some sense to the claim that my chairs are "difficult." For example, I may mean that they are difficult to keep clean. Nevertheless, I do not *imply* that my chairs are difficult when I say that they are hard. So, too, we can wield the second criterion by showing that the "negative" implications are different. Saying that my chair is hard implies that it is not soft, but saying that the examination questions are hard does not imply that they are not soft.

By use of either of the above two criteria, therefore, it can be shown that "hard" is ambiguous when predicated of the subjects, "questions" and "chairs." As a consequence, then—contrary to what Quine asserts—the statement "Some questions and chairs are hard" is meaningless. "Hard" must be used here in one or the other of two different senses; and each of these two senses is appropriate—or makes sense with—one subject, but not the other.

The above would not show, I might add, that the statement "Some questions and chairs are hard" is neither true nor false. If I am right that chairs are not "hard" in the sense that questions are, then, in this sense of "hard," it is true that "Chairs are not hard." But if this latter statement is true, then it is false that "Chairs are hard," again using "hard" in the sense in which it applies only to questions. So, too, if we use "hard" in this same sense, then it is false that "Some questions and chairs are hard." Since this statement is a priori false, it is also meaningless: we do not understand what it would be like for a chair to be "hard" in the same sense in which questions are "hard."

The third criterion discussed in chapter III can also be used, as I tried to demonstrate, to show that "hard" is ambiguous. Instead of repeating the demonstration, it would be more useful to show how this criterion can be applied to a problem that is of some philosophic interest in its own right.

Consider, for example, the problem of determining whether common sense concepts, those which apply to objects of everyday experience, can be meaningfully applied to micro-physical phenomena. Susan Stebbing, in the course of her famous dispute with Eddington, denied that this could be done. She writes:

> No concepts drawn from the level of common-sense thinking are appropriate to sub-atomic, i.e., microphysical, phenomena. Consequently, the language of common sense is not appropriate to the description of such phenomena. Since, however, the man in the street tends to think in pictures and may desire to know something about the latest developments of physics, it is no doubt useful to provide him with some rough picture. The danger arises when the scientist uses the picture for the purpose of making explicit denials, and expresses these denials, in common-sense language used in such a way as to be devoid of sense. This, unfortunately, is exactly what Eddington has done in the passages we are considering, and indeed, in many other passages as well.[21]

We may well agree that Eddington *sometimes* says things that are "devoid of sense," or at least are—if taken literally—very misleading. More specifically, we may agree that Eddington went wrong when he tried to apply *certain* predicates to both macro- and micro-sized objects. For example, it may be a priori false, atlhough I am not asserting that it is, to say that microscopic objects are red. In fact, Eddington himself, although he notes his tendency to think of electrons as being red, and of protons as being neutral grey, admits that this is absurd.[22] Nevertheless, although we may agree with Stebbing on these points, we may still disagree with her *general* contention that it is *always* nonsense to apply common-sense concepts to micro-physical phenomena. If we accept such a general assertion, we have to agree that it is nonsense to apply not only color terms but also such a term as "mass" to electrons; or, at least, we would have to agree that such a term applies to macro- and micro-sized objects only in different senses. Both alternatives are false, however, and can be shown to be so by using our third ambiguity criterion, which can be used not only in proving ambiguity but also in proving univocity. According to this criterion, a term can be used in a single sense with two other terms if it can be used comparatively with these same two terms. A term such as "mass," then,

[21] Susan Stebbing, *Philosophy and the Physicists* (New York: Dover Publications, 1958), p. 51.
[22] *Ibid.*, p. 56n.

can be used in a single sense with terms referring both to macro- and micro-phenomena, for we *can* say meaningfully (and truly) that the mass of an electron at rest is less than that of a baseball. It is also less than that of a star. "Mass" can be applied, therefore, to electrons in the same sense in which it is applied to baseballs and stars. I conclude, then, that Stebbing is wrong in asserting that it is *always* meaningless to apply a concept in a single sense to both macro- and micro-sized objects. It may be nonsense in some cases, but it is not so in all cases.

In the above illustration, I made use of the assumption that the mass of an electron at rest could meaningfully be said to be less than that of a baseball. I do not think that Stebbing would wish to contest this assumption; and if she would, we might buttress the assumption in various ways: for example, by referring to current physical theory. Nevertheless, it must certainly be admitted that the assumption *could* be challenged, even if, ultimately, the challenge could be defeated. In applying this third criterion, moreover, some such assumption must be employed, and such an assumption might very well be challenged. For this reason, use of this third criterion by itself may be inconclusive. To cite one further illustration, suppose we wish to show that it is nonsense to assert that time flows in the same sense in which a river flows. To do this, we might point out that it is meaningless to say, for example, that "Time flows faster than the Mississippi River." Someone who thought it meaningful to speak of the "flow of time," using "flow" as it is used in "the flow of the river," might also think it meaningful to say "Time flows faster than the Mississippi River." Hence, use of our third criterion alone would not be decisive: it would have to be shown, in addition, that the statement about the Mississippi River is also meaningless. A similar point applies to the use of the first two criteria. Someone might deny, for example, that saying that a question is hard implies that it is difficult, or that saying that a chair is hard implies that it is not soft. If so, some further argument would be needed. For this reason, even when one of these three ambiguity criteria can be appealed to in support of a claim of meaninglessness, such an appeal may be insufficient. Additional evidence, or argumentation, may be necessary. Moreover, it should be noted that these criteria, even if of some use, lack the generality of such criteria as the operationalist and verifiability criteria. There would be comparatively few cases in which any of these three criteria would even be applicable. The most I wish to claim, then, is that these criteria may be of *some* use in settling *some* disputes about the meaningfulness of certain statements.

4. Even if we do not have a general test of "meaninglessness" (in the sense of "a priori falsity"), and even if the less general tests described above prove to be of no use, this does not mean that we have no way at all of justifying claims of meaninglessness. We can show that a statement is meaningless by using whatever argument—or kind of argument—is required by the case at hand, instead of using one general argument. For example, one way this might be done is to show that a certain statement implies another statement that is either obviously meaningless or obviously self-contradictory. Take, for example, the assertion "Time began five minutes ago." This statement implies that there was a time, namely, any time earlier than five minutes ago, during which there was no time. This is obviously self-contradictory, for if there was such a time, then it is necessarily false that there was no time during this period. It would be meaningless, then, to say that time began five minutes ago.

Another, but related, way of showing that a statement is meaningless is to show that a necessary presupposition of the statement is itself meaningless or self-contradictory. To cite a controversial example, it has been argued that the statement "Mind and brain are identical" is meaningless because it presupposes that a man's mind is inside his head in the same sense that his brain is. This, in turn, presupposes that, for example, my thought of going to the countryside is somewhere in space (namely, in the space inside my head), which, it is claimed, is obviously meaningless. If so, then the original statement, "Mind and brain are identical," is also meaningless. This example is particularly controversial, for many philosophers would not agree that it is nonsense to assert that "My thought of going to the countryside is somewhere in space." Nevertheless, the general point remains that *if* we could show that the necessary presupposition of the original statement is either meaningless or self-contradictory, then we could show the original statement to be meaningless as well. I do not wish to minimize the difficulty of proving, particularly in any controversial case, that a statement is meaningless. The same difficulty emerges in trying to prove that a statement is either analytically true or self-contradictory. What I am saying, instead, is that the lack of a *general* test of meaninglessness does not mean that we cannot, in some cases, show that a statement is meaningless. We show this by argument, but there are different arguments to be tailored to different cases.

In sum, the lack of a general test of meaninglessness does not mean that the concept is not useful; some statements are obviously meaningless, and for these statements proof is not needed; the three ambiguity criteria I discussed earlier can be of some help in proving meaninglessness; and, even without general criteria, we can prove individual claims of meaninglessness by using various kinds of arguments.

6

I would now like to re-state the theory of meaninglessness I have been proposing, and, in doing so, to summarize some of the main arguments of this book.

I began by distinguishing two skeptical theses—one moderate, one radical—about the use of the concept of "meaninglessness," in the sense in which the term means "neither true nor false." The moderate skeptic holds that all of the standard, general criteria of meaninglessness are defective. The radical skeptic, however, argues that even if we could discover an adequate criterion for the concept of meaninglessness, it would not matter because the concept is hopelessly defective and beyond repair.

I have tried to show, in brief, that the moderate skeptic is right and that the radical skeptic is wrong. The radical skeptic argues that the concept of meaninglessness is flawed, and consequently cannot be used in the way that philosophers have tried to use it because what is meaningless in one language may be meaningful in another language—or what is meaningless at one time may be meaningless at a later time. Also, use of the concept forces us to condemn metaphors, or other figurative uses, which in fact are not meaningless at all. The arguments for each of these claims, as I have tried to demonstrate, are unsound. The basic frailty of these arguments is that they assume that sentences are meaningless, not statements, assertions, propositions, and the like. If this assumption were true—and almost all writers on the subject seem to think that it is—then, the concept of meaninglessness would be of little or no philosophic use. Moreover, this would be true even if the arguments of the radical skeptic were unsound. But such an assumption is not true. We can, despite common arguments to the contrary, speak intelligibly of statements, assertions, and propositions as meaningless. Consequently, we can show that the reasoning of the radical skeptic—and not the concept of meaninglessness—is defective and unworkable.

The thesis of the moderate skeptic, however, fares much better. It is true, as I tried to show in detail, that the standard criteria of meaninglessness—the operationalist, verificationist, and category criteria—are all unreliable. The fact is that we have no reliable, general test of what is "meaningless" (in the sense of "neither true nor false").

That the moderate skeptic is right, however, does not show that we should cease using "meaningless" to mean "neither true nor false." There are other useful concepts for which we lack a general test of their application. Nevertheless, although the reasoning of both moderate and radical skepticism fails to demonstrate that philosophers should repudiate "meaningless" in the sense of "neither true nor false," there are other such reasons. First, there are no statements that are "meaningless" in this sense. Second, once we agree to talk of statements rather than sentences as being meaningless, the rationale for interpreting "meaningless" as "neither true nor false" is eliminated. Third, there is a concept which resembles this sense of "meaninglessness" which can be used for the same essential purposes and does not involve us in the same difficulties as does our employment of the original concept. This second concept is that of a priori falsity.

If we interpret "meaningless" as "a priori false," then the negation of a meaningless statement will be true. For example, if "Virtue is square" is meaningless, then its negation, "Virtue is not square," is true. Thus, we can preserve the rule that the negation of a false statement is true and, conversely, that the negation of a true statement is false. Further, talk of meaningless statements will not force us to abandon the so-called law of the excluded middle (which says that all statements are either true or false).

On this theory, contradictions will be meaningless. But that will not be objectionable, for they will still be false. Both contradictions and other meaningless statements will be meaningless in that we cannot understand what it would be like for them to be true; they will be a priori false. We can understand, for example, what statement is being made when someone asserts that "Some bachelors are unmarried," or that "Virtue is square" by paraphrasing them in terms we do understand (assuming that we do not understand them in the first place). What is not intelligible is what it would be like for such statements to be true.

We can then distinguish contradictions from other meaningless statements by suitably restricting the use of the term "contradiction." If we do this, then the noncontradictory meaningless statements could be described as being synthetic a priori falsehoods. But this is true only on some interpretations of "synthetic a priori." Which interpretation of "synthetic a priori" is chosen, and hence whether or not we describe noncontradictory meaningless statements as synthetic a priori falsehoods, is arbitrary and probably not very important.

One important challenge which might be made to my account of meaninglessness concerns reference-failures. It has been argued by some, notably P. F. Strawson, that reference-failures are statements which are neither true nor false. If he is right, then, contrary to what I have argued, there are at least some statements which are "meaningless" in the sense of "neither true nor false." I have tried to meet this challenge by showing that reference-failures are not statements at all and hence are not statements which are neither true nor false; even if reference-failures were statements, they would not be sufficiently interesting to warrant retaining the old sense of "meaninglessness."

I concluded by discussing ways of proving "meaninglessness," in the sense of "a priori falsehood." My basic contentions were that: we do not need a *general* test of meaninglessness; we can prove meaninglessness in some cases; and some statements are obviously meaningless and in these cases proof of meaninglessness is not needed. Finally, even if we cannot discover any one test of meaninglessness to cover all possible cases—quite probably there is no such test waiting to be discovered—we can still try to develop less powerful tests which will be of some general use but will not apply in all cases. I have tried to contribute to this more modest goal by presenting three criteria of ambiguity which, in turn, may be of some use in settling some disputes about meaninglessness.

index

THE JOHNS HOPKINS PRESS

Designed by Arlene J. Sheer

*Composed in Times Roman text
with Helvetica display*

*Printed on 60-lb. Lock Haven and
bound in Interlaken ARCO Linen
by The Kingsport Press, Inc.*